A Human Relations Guide

By

Donald K. Wright
Alvin Junior College

David D. Field
Thomas Nelson Community College

MSS Information Corporation
655 Madison Avenue, New York, N.Y. 10021

Library of Congress Cataloging in Publication Data

Wright, Donald K
  A human relations guide.

  1. Interpersonal relations. I. Field, David D.,
joint author. II. Title.
HM131.W75   158'.2   72-8998
ISBN 0-8422-0272-2 (pbk)

Copyright © 1972
by MSS Information Corporation
All Rights Reserved

CONTENTS

	INTRODUCTION	5
1.	PROBLEM SOLVING	8
2.	INDIVIDUAL MOTIVATION	20
3.	PERCEPTION, THE GREAT VARIABLE	28
4.	SOME MECHANISMS OF THE MIND	38
5.	CONFORMITY VS NONCONFORMITY	48
6.	WORDS, WORDS, WORDS	55
7.	SOME ASPECTS OF CHANGE	59
8.	DECISION MAKING	63
9.	LEADERSHIP	67
10.	UNDERSTANDING RACIAL DISCRIMINATION	72
11.	EFFECTIVE HUMAN RELATIONS: GUIDELINES	85
	FOOTNOTES	87
	GLOSSARY	89
	BIBLIOGRAPHY	91

INTRODUCTION

A course in human relations should not emphasize the memorization of data provided by the instructor or contained in the reference material. Rather, the primary objective should be to positively influence the attitudes and the outlooks of class members who in turn, it is hoped, will influence others. Although man has long been concerned with the many problems involving interpersonal relationships, it has only been in recent years that attempts have been made to explore these problems and search for solutions to them in formalized classroom settings. Psychology, sociology and anthropology courses have long been offered in American colleges, and each in its own way has been concerned with man and his behavior. However, it has only been within the past 20 to 30 years that courses in human relations have become a part of college curriculums and there are many institutions of higher learning which as of this date still do not offer such courses.

Courses in human relations arose out of two basic demands on our educational system. The first had to do with the need for a course which would cut across subject boundaries using elements from each to study the total person and the total environment in which he lives. Thus the student of human relations must be able to use the concepts from all the behavioral sciences (which is itself a relatively new term) and from any of the natural sciences (such as biology) when necessary. The second is based on the belief that today more than ever before, educational institutions have an obligation to raise questions and provide answers whenever possible in the field of human problems. These problems must be approached with the same dedication and thoroughness which have characterized the efforts of the natural scientists and which have achieved such spectacular results.

The term human relations may be defined in several ways. One of the simplest is contained in the statement that it is a study of how people should get along with other people. This is a very general definition and yet it is very accurate. Another might be that human relations is the achieving of harmony and the avoidance of discord among individuals and groups. Here it should be noted that the word "discord" should not be confused with the word "conflict." Conflict in interpersonal relations is both natural and to some extent desirable. It is only when conflict becomes destructive that it impedes man's progress. It is hoped that the student of human relations would be able to gain insight into his own behavior and that of others. He should then be able to develop functional skills which would assist him in associating harmoniously with his fellows.

The question arises as to whether the study of human relations is a science or an art. This will be further scrutinized in the chapter dealing with the scientific method. A course in human relations is basically concerned with three components: people, problems and the solution of these problems. As we observe man down through the centuries, we cannot escape the fact that he has faced and is facing major problems of every description which seem to originate in his inability to live in peaceful coexistance with his fellow man. It is also apparent that although he can solve the most complex problems involving physical or material factors (such as placing a man on the moon) he seems incapable of solving those problems which involve his feelings or emotions. Witness examples of this in our long history of warfare, crime, labor disputes, family disintegration and individual maladjustment.

The age in which we live has been described by some as a Golden Age because of the economic affluence and technological success which modern man has achieved. On the other hand, in spite of our material progress, we are not fully reaping the benefits of our inventiveness. Indeed, instead of being a truly Golden Age, it might more accurately be described as an age of despair. Consider the fact that the second most prevalent cause of death among college students in the United States today is suicide. It might be even more significant to consider that the first cause is accidents resulting from the use (or misuse) of one of our most essential inventions, the automobile. Further, consider the symptoms of dispair so evident today among those in all age groups who have choosen the route of alcohol and drugs as an escape from reality.

Cultural lag is apparent on every hand. While man has made great progress materially, he remains in the stone age as far as his interpersonal relationships are concerned. It is the purpose of this guide to examine some problems in human relations and discuss possible solutions. The case study method will be used when appropriate. These cases, while varied insofar as the situations are concerned, emphasize certain broad concepts which may be useful in real-life problems. Some of these cases are based on factual situations while others are fictional. All of them have been prepared by the writers or by students who have previously been enrolled in human relations courses at Thomas Nelson Community College.

One concept that is probably of primary importance is that most, if not all, problems in human relations are caused by certain attitudes which individuals possess and which are in opposition to the attitudes of others with whom they come in contact. Thus, there is the need for a change in attitudes if the problem is to be avoided in the first place or resolved once it occurs. This leads to the extremely vital question, can people, especially adults, change their attitudes? If the answer to this question is "no," then the hope for the future of mankind is indeed dim. If, on the other hand, the answer is "yes," perhaps there is hope and perhaps we will be able to someday have a world in which we are as successful in our interpersonal relationships as we have been in those involving the material aspects of life.

CHAPTER ONE

PROBLEM SOLVING

Human beings today find themselves surrounded by problems. The foreman, the superintendent, the school teacher or administrator, the parent, the husband, the wife, the military leader, the businessman in short all of us are confronted with problems for which solutions must be found if our lives or the routine of the group with which we are associated are to proceed as trouble free as possible. A recent advertisement by a firm of personnel consultants had this to say about people and problems.

"YOUR COMPANY HAS NO PEOPLE PROBLEMS? Well, maybe... but most companies do... of one kind or another.

Turnover. Tardiness. Trouble attracting good people. Absenteeism. Union troubles. Low morale. Poor motivation. Inefficiency. Racial unrest. Resentments. Poor supervision. Poor communication. If your company doesn't have one or more of these problems now, it will. There's no avoiding them. They come with people.

But smart company executives know they can be solved- even prevented. They know there's no substitute for experienced, professional help. Professionals know what to look for to pinpoint, analyze and resolve them."[1]

It is indeed a truism that we as individuals spend much of our time trying to resolve perplexing situations which have arisen due to human behavior. Perhaps by talking about problem solving we are taking the wrong approach. Perhaps we should devote ourselves to problem avoidance so that we then would limit that which we have to solve. The comparison might be made to the old and the new concept in fire fighting. Years ago the fire department was called only after the fire had started. Today modern fire science teaches that most of the department's time should be spend in fire prevention, thus eliminating many of the fires before they have a chance to begin. In the field of human relations we know that the prevention of conflict is most desirable but we also know that in spite of our best efforts problems will arise. Of course, we are hopeful that the concepts discussed in a human relations class will serve a twofold purpose. Just as the fire department can prevent some fires from starting, so instruction in human relations may not only provide individuals with the means of solving existing or potential problems, but this same instruction may serve to reduce the number of problems which an individual might face.

Problems which confront man may be classified in two broad categories. The first might be called the physical problems. An example might be that of placing a man on the moon. In 1961, John F. Kennedy stated that before the end of the decade, the United States would succeed in accomplishing this goal. The problems were perhaps as difficult and variable as any which man had previously faced in the field of science. Money was appropriated, the best qualified experts were organized, facilities were established and the work began. By a concerted effort involving billions of dollars and millions of man-hours, all problems involved were solved and on July 20, 1969, two men made what they termed "one small step for man but one giant stride for man-kind" as they stepped out of their space craft onto a surface never before touched by humans. Reports from the men involved indicate that one year later they had feelings of great disappointment. As far as they could ascertain, mankind has not taken much of a stride as a result of their historic feat. While their footsteps remain imprinted on the face of the moon, here on earth there are the ugly footprints of poverty, illiteracy, crime, war, drug addiction and countless other social problems. All of this is an excellent example of the phenomenon known as social or cultural lag. While man is able to make fantastic progress in the physical realm, today he faces as many or perhaps more social problems than at any other time in his history.

One of the most challenging books written since World War II is entitled "The Proper Study of Mankind." It is the work of Stuart Chase and its title is taken from the often quoted lines by Alexander Pope in his famous *Essay on Man*. In this essay Pope says "Know then thyself, presume not God to scan; the proper study of mankind is man."

Among other topics discussed by Chase is that of problem solving. He states that there are six methods by which man can solve a problem.[2] These may apply to both those of a physical or purely human nature. He also points out that the six methods may overlap. Here they are as listed by Chase:

1. Appeal to the supernatural.
2. Appeal to worldly authority-the older the better.
3. Intuition.
4. Common sense.
5. Pure logic.
6. The scientific method.

Let us take a look at each one of these methods. Appeals to the supernatural have been a part of mankind's problem solving devices as far back as history has been recorded. Even the most primitive peoples believed in the existence of supernatural powers, or gods, which would protect them if they were worthy, and punish them if unworthy. These unseen powers would also respond to requests for help and thus solve problems facing the people concerned. The culture of the American Indians provides an excellent example of this type of problem solving. If the absence of rain threatened the survival of the tribe, certain rain dances and other ceremonies were performed. If the problem was one of a possible attack by another tribe, the supernatural powers controlling war were asked for help and guidance. In the matter of personal illness and when earthly cures failed, again various gods were appealed to for assistance. Here the route of appeal might have been through a worldly authority - the medicine man or witch doctor. In many parts of the world today such primitive appeals to the supernatural are a part of everyday problem solving. More civilized man, on the other hand, has a more organized method of appeal based on his religious convictions. It is interesting to note that one of the common elements found in any culture is the existence of some form of religious worship.

Today whether the individual be Protestant, Jew, Moslem, Hindu, Buddhist or a believer in any other faith, he has open to him at all times a method of asking for solution to his problems. Thus the mother who fears for the life of her sick child, the wife who is concerned for the safety of her husband in Vietnam, the husband who is facing a personal crises in his marriage, the businessman who has financial problems or any other individual who has faith in an all powerful God finds strength and possibly a solution through the process of prayer. Although there are many today who might discount prayer as a practical solution to problems, there are many who will testify to its effectiveness. This group not only includes those people who we might describe as "religious" but would also include many psychologists and psychiatrists who recognize the therapeudic value of recognizing the problem and releasing one's feelings concerning it. Purely from the psychological point of view there is some benefit to be derived from the act of praying, and, in the case of a Roman Catholic, the practice of confession. These religious (supernatural) acts are at least steps in the direction of problem solving even though they may not always meet with success.

The next method according to Chase is the appeal to a worldly authority. This, of course, is a very common procedure. The child with a problem takes it to one or both of his parents. On the other hand this same child, if he is of school age, may choose to see one of the guidance counselors or a favorite teacher. Husbands and wives with problems may seek solutions from a variety of sources. If it is a financial problem there is the bank or the loan company. If it is a physical problem, there is the doctor. If it is one involving the preservation of their marriage, there is the marriage counselor or the psychiatrist. The individual on the job may seek the solution from his foreman. The foreman goes to his supervisor and so on. In many cases human problems become so difficult and so serious that appeals are made to the courts. One only has to think of the many problems involving civil rights which defied solution on a person to person or group to group basis. Inevitably these problems were taken to the various law-making agencies in our government including the United States Congress. When it became evident that the passage of certain laws did not solve the problems, the next step was to the courts where many of the issues had to be finally resolved by the highest tribunal in the land, the U. S. Supreme Court. Certainly appealing to human authority is an important aspect of problem solving. However, it should be recognized that such appeals take place only after the problem has arisen. How much better it would be if these problems could be avoided in the first place!

Intuition is the next method. This is an interesting approach and one which is difficult to explain. Intuition may be defined as a feeling which directs us to act in a certain manner or which reveals to us certain events yet to occur. For some reason we seem to ascribe this intuitive ability to women more so than to men. Indeed it is not uncommon to hear reference to a "woman's intuition" as if it were much more reliable than that possessed by a man. Many times we hear individuals with a problem make the statement that they have arrived at a solution but with no apparent reason. They state that they will take a course of action just because they "have a feeling" that it is the correct course to take. When pressed for a more definitive reason, they cannot provide one and simply repeat that they just have a feeling or a "hunch." Are such feelings or hunches actually intuition or has the person arrived at a solution by some decision making process of which he is not aware? In other words, is so-called intuition actually based on a form of reasoning? Another consideration in discussing intuition is the working of law of averages. If a person repeatedly has hunches or intuitive thoughts concerning certain problems or events, he is bound to be right at least once in awhile. On these occasions he is quite ready to proclaim his powers of intuition while conveniently forgetting all those cases when his hunches did not produce results. This is easy to see in the example of the mother who is anxious to hear from her son or daughter who is far from home and perhaps facing certain difficulties. The mother tells her husband that her intuition tells her that the child will call that evening. The child does not call. The next day the mother makes the same comment. Again no call. After a few days the call does come and the mother is able to exclaim triumphantly that her intuition never fails her. Of course, she not only disregards the days when there was no call but she also ignores the fact that sooner or later the child is probably going to call anyway.

Before leaving the subject of intuition it is extremely important to state that we must not discard its use in the realm of problem solving. Regardless of how it develops in a person, we can say that it does have value in many areas. Even in the laboratory where the natural scientist must strive for objectivity, one cannot rule out the possibility that intuition may have a part to play. In fact the history of scientific experimentation is full of examples where the researcher has applied certain techniques or taken certain actions based on nothing more than his intuition. To put it another way, he has taken certain actions which might at the time seemed to have lacked a scientific basis! In many cases the one step taken intuitively has provided the key to the problem at hand. Again, however, we must ask why he took this action. Was it actually intuition or was it the result of some rational process so deep in the mind of the scientist as to emerge under the guise of intuition? Although we cannot answer this question with authority, we might summarize by stating that intuition is a method of problem solving and that regardless of its nature or its origin, it often seems to work at least to the satisfaction of the person involved and this after all may be the only important criterion.

Roger J. Williams, one of the world's outstanding biochemists, has this to say about intuition, "In our own day intuition is of tremendous value in the fields of business and human relations. Some men have an almost uncanny ability to pick winners. Some know intuitively what is likely to happen. If it is something bad they may say, 'I smell a rat.' of course, they don't literally smell anything, but the messages from the outside world which come to them by way of nerve receptors are interpreted as being similar to a bad odor.

The value of intuitions depends on whose intuitions they are. If it were possible in science, business, politics or religion to select those with the highest intuitive powers, this would mark a big advance. A nationally prominent businessman with many diverse successes to his credit, told me, 'When you are fifty-five percent sure, it is time to act. If you wait until you are ninety-five percent sure, the show is over."[3]

The next method of problem solving is through the application of common sense. Immediately we are confronted with a problem of definition. What is common sense? The term is used extensively but it is suspected that the user has his own understanding as to what it means. More importantly he probably has his own opinion as to who possesses this apparently desirable quality. We hear such comments as, "He is a wonderful person and highly educated, but he lacks common sense." Another frequent statement is, "All the education in the world is not worth much if the person does not have common sense." It is interesting to note that most people believe that they are endowed with this attribute but that in their opinion, there are many who do not have it. If common sense were an effective method of problem solving, and if everyone who thinks he possesses it actually did, it should follow that there should be few problems left to solve. Keith Davis in <u>Human Relations at Work</u> has an interesting comment which is relevant. "If effective human relations is just common sense, why is it so scarce - so uncommon? Why is it so difficult to use? Why was it not generally adopted by managers fifty years ago? Surely they had common sense. If experience is the proper teacher of human relations, a given quantity of experience should provide a given quantity of skill; but this is hardly so. A few persons become skilled at human relations through experience, but most do not. Human relations requires the learning of technical knowledge about human behavior, development of social skills, development of analytical frameworks, and research into conditions which affect each situation."

Like intuition, common sense is usually described as something a person has acquired in some unknown manner. However, unlike intuition, most of us think we can recognize individuals who have common sense. To further complicate the situation, we find that other words and phrases are used to describe a person who is supposed to have common sense. We say that he is "down to earth" or that he has "both feet on the ground." We might also say that he is "practical," "realistic," "direct," or "uncomplicated." The point is that although we use the term common sense and may know what it means to us, it is an extremely subjective term and one which does not lend itself to the exactness we would like to achieve in our approach to problem solving.

Pure logic is the fifth method mentioned by Chase. It is important to note that he uses the adjective "pure." To some there might be a close relationship between common sense and logic. However, the logic we are referring to here can be defined with some degree of accuracy. Pure logic is based on the use of the syllogism. The traditional example of the correct use of this device is as follows:

```
            A        B
   1.   All men are mortal.
            C        A
   2.   Socrates is a man.
                         C         B
   3.   (Therefore) Socrates is mortal.
```

In a syllogism each part is identified. Statement number one is the major premise. This must be a universal truth which can be accepted by everyone without further proof or explanation. The next part (2) is the minor premise. It is likewise acceptable as true without question but it is a narrower statement of the truth. In other words the minor premises does not apply universally but rather to a smaller group or to an individual or object as the case might be. The third part is called the conclusion. The conclusion is reached by means of a rigid formula expressed as follows:

```
A - B
C - A
C - B
```

It would appear that this method should provide us with an excellent problem solving device, however, it has some shortcomings which make it difficult to apply in the field of human relations. The major difficulty is in achieving agreement on the major premise. For example there are some individuals who would hold that the following premises are true:

All Mexicans are lazy.
All bosses lack understanding.
All union members are selfish.
All Japanese are cruel.

Such statements as these are often at the base of the problem at hand. Thus the logical reasoning can go no further because there is no way to eliminate the feelings, emotions and prejudices of the individual concerned purely with the use of logic.

Another shortcoming in the use of pure logic is that it assumes that all human beings will be willing to make use of this method when in actuality we find very few people in matters of personal relationships able to take such an objective look at a situation. Often one party to an argument will entreat the other individual to "be logical." What he really means is "accept my position as correct." However, the other person probably thinks he is being logical and it is the first party who is being illogical. Although these weaknesses exist in the use of pure logic as a problem solving procedure, this does not mean that we are eliminating the need for logical thinking. Such thinking is, of course, very desirable if we can apply it to a situation without allowing our preconceived attitudes to dominate.

Finally Chase offers the scientific method as a means of solving problems. Certainly this method has achieved consistent results in the field of the natural sciences. Through the use of this method man has been able to approach a problem in an analytical and objective manner. The research technician properly using this method eliminates the possibility that bias will influence the outcome of his work. This method when correctly used forces the individual to be honest in his findings. The scientist may fervently hope that the outcome of an experiment will prove the hypothesis he so carefully developed, but if the experiments fail, he has no choice but to admit that either his hypothesis was incorrect or something went wrong with his procedures. The scientific method can be outlined as follows:

1. A problem exists.

2. All available facts concerning the problem are accumulated.

3. An hypothesis is developed. (This is an assumption which seems to be true.)

4. Through experimentation the hypothesis is either proved or disproved.

5. If the hypothesis has been proven, we can make valid predictions concerning future situations.

Let us cite some examples from history. Europeans during the time of Columbus had a problem. They were not able to reach the Orient by land as they had in the past due to the existence of hostile groups along the trade routes. Trade with the Far East was considered essential to the economy and comfort of the people of Europe. Columbus over a period of time devoted himself to the solution of this problem. He assembled as many facts as he possible could and came to the conclusion that the earth was not flat as it appeared, but that it was actually a globe. He then hypothesized that if the world was round, he could reach the East by sailing West. Now he would have to prove this through experimentation. Columbus could only make one conclusive experiment and that was to start his voyage into the unknown area far beyond the western horizon. The fact that he did not arrive in the Orient is not important in this instance. He had proved that the world was not flat and he actually thought he had reached his objective. Now it was possible to make predictions based on his findings. In every case, without exception, a person starting in one direction will eventually return to his starting point.

Thousands of other examples could be given to illustrate the operation of the scientific method as a problem solving device in the field of natural sciences. The history of medical progress reveals the validity of experimentation. Just one example will suffice. The problem was the existence of the dreaded disease of yellow fever in the tropics. There were many suspected causes of this killer but none could be substantiated until a young army doctor by the name of Walter Reed assembled enough facts to hypothesize that the cause was a germ carried by mosquitos which had bitten a person already infected. In this particular case the experimentation was drastic in that human beings were used as subjects. Soldiers volunteered to allow themselves to be bitten by the mosquitos. In due time they developed the disease and in fact some of them died because at that time there was no method of treatment. Now that the cause of the disease was established, steps could be taken to prevent it from occurring. As mentioned, this was an extremely unusual use of the scientific method in that humans were used rather than animals.

Let us briefly summarize the most significant aspects of the scientific method. If used properly, it eliminates the feelings and preconceived ideas of the individual performing the research. Next, and this is of utmost importance, if successful, it makes it possible for the scientist to predict with great accuracy (100% in most cases) what will happen if certain conditions exist. For example if two parts of hydrogen and one part of oxygen are mixed at sea level the result will be water every time. Or if, while standing on the earth, an object which is heavier than air is released, it will always fall to the ground. The law of gravity so directs. The scientific method makes it possible for man to predict the orbits of satellites and to pinpoint the place of landing for returning astrounauts. Without the scientific method, we would not have achieved the technological progress which is ours.

Now let us discuss the scientific method with respect to problems which develop among human beings. One such problem is the existence of crime. Not only does crime exist as never before, but there is every indication that the crime rate is increasing. Man has long faced this problem but without solution. Our entire penal system is based on the idea that if we punish (through imprisonment) or if we rehabilitate (through prison training programs) we will reduce the amount of crime. It is obvious that such has not been the case. Back in the 19th Century an Italian by the name of Lombroso (1836-1909) was concerned about this problem. He sought its solution through use of the scientific method. After gathering what he believed were the available facts, he developed an hypothesis. He stated that most individuals become criminals because they possessed certain inherited physical traits. These were apparent in the size and shape of the person's skull, forehead, jaw, ears and other features. In what he thought was a scientific procedure, he began to catalog all known criminals with respect to the traits he had established as significant. Although his theory gained some degree of acceptability, it could never be proven. In fact it was found that many criminals did not have the traits Lombroso described, while many individuals (including the police inspector according to some accounts) who were definitely not criminals possessed the specified characteristics. Even today we have little or no exact knowledge concerning the causation of crime. If Lombroso's theory had been correct, we could have predicted who the criminals would be and taken steps to either remove them from society or give them preventive training. Obviously this is not the case.

The problem of applying the scientific method to human behavior is extremely complex. Often we are not even able to go beyond the first step as we cannot agree on a statement of the problem. For example while many might say that juvenile delinquency is a problem, an equal number might say that the real problem is delinquent parents or adults. Even after we isolate the problem, it is difficult to ascertain all the facts. In working with inanimate objects such as missiles and rockets it is possible to gather all known facts. In dealing with human beings it is impossible to have available all necessary information. Further difficulties are encountered when we reach the experimental step in the scientific method. How can we experiment with human beings? A recent press dispatch relates to this problem.[4] Dr. Arnold Hutschnecker, a psychiatrist acting as a consultant to the President's Commission on Violence has proposed that "all the nation's children between six and eight undergo Rorschach (ink blot) tests and a test based on sociological and psychological data to 'detect the children who have violent and homicidal tendencies.' Corrective treatment could begin at that time." Dr. Hutschnecker apparently believes that potential criminals can be detected by testing. This in itself is debatable. For the sake of argument, however, let us assume that he is correct in this assumption. Now the government proposes to begin testing all six to eight year old children in the nation. Immediately there would be raised a question as to the constitutionality of such a procedure. Further can you imagine the reaction from parents. How many would want their child to be tested in this manner and perhaps identified as a potential criminal? How many would consent to have their children under some "corrective treatment?" Finally what assurance would there be that the treatment would be effective? In this example, as in all other examples concerning human behavior, we encounter many important considerations which limit the application of the scientific method. Perhaps the three most vital are those which concern causation, experimentation and the prediction of human behavior. In the natural sciences causes of reactions may be complicated, but in time they are usually identified and explained. A computer is a complex piece of equipment, the operation of which almost defies our imagination. However, a person trained in computer technology can explain what makes the computer compute. In the realm of human behavior how can we ever explain with any degree of reliability the actions of individuals? Why does the honest and trusted employee of the building and loan company become an embezzler? Why does the faithful husband and father leave one day never to return? Why does the "all American" type boy attack and strangle the neighbor's small child? On and on we go. Even a trained psychiatrist or psychologist can only make educated guesses in arriving at the reasons for an individual's behavior.

As for the experimental step, social scientists are at a distinct disadvantage when compared to their counterparts in the natural sciences. These latter investigators are able to arrange planned experiments in which they use either material substances or animals. The social scientist's interest is in the behavior of people thus it would be desirable to conduct experiments with people in controlled conditions. However, there are some basic reasons why this is not always possible. People cannot be used in those cases where the procedures might be considered immoral, illegal or harmful to the subjects. While it is true that there have been isolated examples of experimentation with people, the social scientist is still bound by many considerations which do not affect the natural scientist. At the present time the team of Masters and Johnson is conducting extensive research in the field of human sexual behavior and although they are careful to obtain the consent of the people being used, they have been the target of much criticism by those in our society who view such activities as immoral.

Thus it can be seen that those social experiments which have been and will be conducted, are by their nature limited in scope and do not in reality attack the most serious problems which face us today. For example, we probably have enough genetic information available so that the physical scientist and the social scientist working together could use it to improve the physical characteristics and the behavior of man through selective breeding. Cattlemen have done this for years as have the developers of new and better varieties of vegetables, fruits and flowers. Why then don't we begin a scientific breeding program which would improve the human species and thus perhaps eliminate some of the problems (such as mental retardation) which exist? The answer is obvious. Our cultural environment is such that most people would not accept such a proposal.

Final, there is the problem of prediction. As has been stated, the natural scientist is able to make accurate predictions once he has proven his hypothesis, but how can social scientists predict human behavior? Human beings are so complex and subject to such a multiplicity of causative factors that each individual is unique and thus his behavior is unpredictable. In spite of this we believe that some prediction is possible in the human field. For example, in recent years with the help of surveys and computers, election results have been forecast with a high degree of accuracy. But, and this is most important, they are not always correct as evidenced by the 1970 elections in England where it was the unanimous opinion of experts that Mr. Wilson would be reelected. When the returns were counted, much to the embarrassment of the "experts," Mr. Wilson was defeated and Mr. Heath was the new Prime Minister.

To carry the example of the elections one step further, it should also be remembered that even though we may be able to predict the outcome of the election, we would be at a loss to predict the way in which <u>individuals</u> will vote. This difficulty can also be seen in another example. If we attended a Harvard-Yale football game we could predict with a high degree of certainty that if Yale made a touchdown, the spectators on the Yale side of the field would jump up, cheer and otherwise express their elation. But, would everyone on the Yale side react in this manner? Probably not. Even a staunch Yale rooter might under some circumstance remain seated and not even open his mouth when his team scored. To summarize, it might be said that we can in some cases predict crowd reaction, but not with scientific accuracy. Further, and this is most important, the ability to correctly predict the actions of specific individuals is extremely limited. If we could predict human behavior with certainty, we would then perhaps avoid most of the problems we face in the realm of interpersonal relationships. Unhappy marriages would be impossible. Drug addiction and alcoholism would be eliminated. Crime would no longer exist and the potential suicide would be identified and given treatment. We would have closed the gap which exists between the physical and the social sciences.

Perhaps the day will come when we will be able to use the scientific method completely in finding solutions to mankind's most perplexing social problems. That day is not in the foreseeable future. In the meantime one of our greatest hopes lies in the expansion of human relations training. If individuals can develop skills which will lead to insight into their own behavior and that of others, the result should be an improvement in human relationships. As knowledge is gained concerning needs and patterns of behavior, the degree of predictability may be increased giving us a better chance of controlling future events. Each person may in effect become a "predicting agent" and thus be able to contribute to better social harmony which is our eventual goal.

CHAPTER TWO

INDIVIDUAL MOTIVATION

In discussing individual motivation, we are entering an area in which we would like to have much more information than is presently available. Although we can generalize about the reasons behind human behavior, we have a much more difficult time when we attempt to be specific. If we could isolate causes, we might be able to better control our own behavior and that of others.

A.H.Maslow has divided the factors in human motivation into five categories and arranged them schematically in the form of a pyramid. At the base are those physiological urges which are recognized as universal factors in man's behavior. Those which are most apparent are the drives of hunger, thirst, fatigue and sex. There are others, but for the purpose of illustration, these four will suffice. Each of these drives is essential for survival. Man must eat, drink, rest and reproduce if he is to live as an individual and if he is to insure the perpetuation of the group. Much of man's life is devoted directly or indirectly to satisfying these physiological needs. Many primitive groups had little time for anything else but meeting basic life needs. This is true even today among some primitive tribes. The Aruntas who inhabit the wastes of Australia must spend most of their time and energy in search of food and water. Their rest periods, while essential to the continuation of the quest for sustenance, are minimal. They rarely remain in one spot for long and thus have never established permanent dwellings or living areas. While sex is essential to the group survival and a source of individual gratification just as it is in civilized societies, it remains a basic bodily function without the embellishments which have been attached to it in more sophisticated cultures.

In contrast to the ways of the primitive, civilized man, while still concerned with the fundamental needs and the security they bring, does not have to spend as much time in search of these basics and is thus able to devote more energy to other pursuits. This is obvious when we consider the dramatic reduction in the average work week. In the last 50 years workers have gone from a work week of about 60 hours to one of 40 or less thus increasing the amount of leisure time available. Modern man can earn enough money to provide himself with security (the second item in Maslow's pyramid) in much less time than it took his forefathers.

Modern man has another group of needs which may be referred to as social or psychological. This does not mean that primitive people do not also have these needs. In all cultures individuals desire the approval of their fellows and actively seek to obtain it. However, in the past this was usually obtained by excelling in those activities which were closely related to the basic biological needs. Thus the male Indian who was the mightiest hunter, trapper or warrior was held in high esteem by other tribe members. Likewise the woman with the most domestic skill and knowledge held a place of respect in the group. Today individuals seek the satisfaction of their social needs in countless ways. They may join various clubs, participate in competative sports, strive for financial success or adopt and support causes which will bring them the satisfaction they desire. Although Maslow (and others) recognize social needs, there are some psychologists who would argue that everything we do in one way or another, consciously or unconsciously, is related to the satisfaction of our physiological drives. Thus the individual who is active in the civic organization, while apparently motivated by the desire to serve the community, may actually be insuring that he develop good "contacts" so that he will obtain more customers for his business (or more clients if he is a lawyer) and thus make more money with which to insure that his basic biological needs are met.

In addition to the social needs, man has certain ego needs which influence his behavior. The desire to be treated as an individual is a strong force in our interpersonal relationships. We like the sound of our name and resent being referred to in impersonal terms. In this age of computers, social security numbers, bank account numbers, zip codes, area codes and general automation, there seems to be a tendency in both government and business to regard people as numbers rather than as people. This can be very deflating and even degrading. It can be said that much of the resentment which built up in the southern negros was the traditional reference regardless of their age and station in life as "boy" or "girl." Probably the most dehumanizing experience an individual can suffer today is to become a convict. Here the man is placed in a mold. Not only is his very appearance altered to fit the pattern, but he actually becomes a number and is treated as such. One of the writers was recently part of a group which visited one of the largest Federal penitentiaries in which a very prominent individual was an inmate. As we entered the large dining hall, one of the group asked our guide if he could point out this particular prisoner. The guide very candidly replied that prison personnel made it a point never to identify individual prisoners and that even if he wanted to, he would not be able to designate the man in question. The current unrest in our prisons is probably related to this complete loss of ego which prisoners must undergo as part of our penal system. It might also be noted that many men going into the armed forces experience a similar reaction as they are regimented into the military way of life. The Army, Navy and Air Force have recognized this recently and are attempting to change the traditional concepts and insure that the individual does not feel a loss of dignity or self esteem when he becomes a member of the military forces.

One of the sometimes overlooked dangers of the population explosion is that with the increase in the number of people in the world, more impersonal treatment seems to result.

As we analyze the behavior of people, it is apparent that many of them act the way they do because they are primarily interested in the psychological needs which are part of their personality. The term "self actualization" can be applied to man's attempt to develop his potential to the utmost thus giving him a feeling of accomplishment. This seems to be an important factor in the behavior of human beings. People want to be treated with respect. Most of us strive to reach a position where we will gain this status. This does not mean that we have to have respect, admiration and acclaim on a large scale. Few of us can gain this measure of success. It does mean that in the family, at work or among our associates we crave the respect which we feel we deserve as human beings. In analyzing the behavior of Lee Harvey Oswald, it is important to note that his personality and self image were strongly and adversely affected by the fact his wife not only questioned his manhood privately, but also did so in the presence of other people. Could this be one reason why he obtained a gun and allegedly killed President Kennedy? Was this his way of showing his wife, and the world, that he was indeed a man? Public humiliation is dangerous. It is trite but true to say that we should praise openly but criticise in private. Too often this precept is disregarded and the results can be extremely harmful to both the individual and the group.

The desire to be accepted by the group, the desire to be treated as an individual rather than as a cog in a machine and the desire for respect are all important in determining human behavior. Because man is a gregarious animal, he seeks the companionship of others. Even though an indivudal realizes that he is limited in his education, leadership ability, social background or economic position, he seeks the acceptance of some individual or group. This becomes apparent early in life. It becomes especially noticeable and important when the individual reaches adolescence. Peer approval is one of the dominent factors in the life of young people and nothing is more devastating or emotionally distressing than to be "put down" or "cut off" by the group. For most people this feeling continues in varying degrees into adult life.

If we learned anything from the famous Hawthorne studies, it was that above everything else the workers in the various plants valued their status as human beings and responded favorably when that status was recognized. Conversely when individuals are not treated with the respect they believe they deserve, there is a decline in morale and a loss in efficiency. As mentioned previously, perhaps the major concept to keep in mind when considering human motivation is that of multiple causation. It is difficult, if not impossible, to isolate the precise cause of a human being's actions. We are too complex and so is our environment to provide easy answers to the question of motivation.

It is not our purpose to discuss all the many theories of motivation which have been developed. To just summarize them would take an entire volume. However, we will briefly describe some of the more interesting and important theories which have been developed.

For centuries there have been attempts to establish a cause and effect relationship between a person's physical traits and his behavior. Most of these attempts have been based on subjective impressions rather than on scientific procedures. Fiction writers have consistantly related the physical appearance of their characters with their actions. Shakespeare described Cassius as having a "lean and hungry look" and made it clear that his behavior was in keeping with his physique. Another character made famous by Shakespeare was Falstaff who was fat and jovial. Dr.Jeckyl was handsome, well groomed and exemplary in his behavior, however, when he became the hideous Mr. Hyde, he behaved accordingly.

We have already referred to Lombroso's attempts to explain criminal behavior in terms of physical attributes and indicated that his work has been discredited. The search for a connection between the physical and the behavioral continues however, and is exemplified in the work of W. H. Sheldon who presented (1949) a classification of humans based on body types. The endomorph is round, soft and fat (Falstaff). The ectomorph is thin, angular and boney (Cassius) while the mesomorph is muscular, well built and athletic (Dr. Jeckyl). According to Sheldon, body types help determine the behavior and the personality of the individual. While this theory is accepted to a degree by some authorities,there are many who do not believe that it has been scientifically verified.

Another approach to the subject of human behavior can be found in the work of those scientists (psychologists) who offer the phenomenon of conditioning as the answer to motivation. Two distinct types of conditioning are recognized and can be easily demonstrated. The first is called "classical conditioning" and was pioneered by the Russian scientist Pavlov in his classic experiments with dogs. Pavlov reduced the behavior of organism to a stimulus-response (S-R) relationship. He and his followers held that every action (R) must have a cause (S) and every cause (S) must have an action (R). As the bell (S) rings signalling the end of class, the students arise from their seats and leave the room(). The S-R concept was known to man (not necessarily by those terms) long before Pavlov, but his special contribution was to bring a new dimension to the relationship. He was able to have an organism respond to a stimulus with a response which would normally not be expected. Thus if he presented food to a dog, the dog's saliva glands would produce more saliva preparatory to chewing the food. Pavlov noted that this salivation would begin before the actual presentation of the food. When the dog was aware that the individual bearing the food was approaching, his salivation would increase. Pavlov then arranged what must certainly be one of the most referred to psychological experiments in history. He coupled a sound (tone) with the presentation of the food. Of course, the dog's saliva glands became active. After several such presentations the sound alone was presented without the food. The salivation took place just as it had when the food was present. The term "conditioned response" has been given to this phenomenon. The organism can be "conditioned" to respond in a manner not normally expected. Note that the response was inevitable and beyond the control of the organism. The implications of this are vast. Humans can be conditioned in an almost endless number of ways. Our daily lives are filled with examples of classical conditioning. Many of the reactions we experience while driving a car are the results of conditioning. Why should we apply our brakes at a red light, but drive through when the light is green? The answer is obvious when we understand Pavlovian conditioning.

There is another form of conditioning which is also extremely important in considering the reason people behave the way they do. This is referred to as "operant conditioning." B. F. Skinner is regarded as the foremost authority in this area and his work has done much to establish the validity of such conditioning. Whereas Pavlov's dog had no choice in his response (salivating), Skinner's experimental subjects (usually pigeons) do have a choice of sorts. Operant conditioning results when the organism <u>learns</u> to make a response. A hungry animal placed in a cage will explore the environment in his search for food or as a result of his natural curiosity. If in his random exploration he presses a lever which in turn causes a pellet of food to be released into the cage, the animal has taken the first step in conditioning. It will not be too long before he will go directly to the lever, press it and thus obtain the food he needs. Again this is not something which began with Skinner. Animal (and child) trainers have made use of this principal for centuries. The horse, dog, elephant, lion or child which performs a certain desired act on command receives a reward (reinforcement). Observe the animal acts in a circus and you will see the trainer rewarding each performance with some desirable tid-bit.

Operant conditioning is certainly a major factor in the motivation of human beings. Napoleon said that a man would go through hell for a little piece of ribbon to wear on his uniform. Modern armies make use of ribbons and medals to motivate men to fight and to die if necessary. Of course, the ribbon is only the symbol of the acclaim, but it is still a reinforcement.

Another explanation of human behavior can be found in the psychoanalytical theory. Sigmund Freud (1856-1939), acknowledged as the father of modern psychiatry, believed that all human behavior could be explained by means of this theory. To Freud human behavior was related to unseen and subconscious forces which are deep within our beings. He believed that our personalities and actions are directed by three factors which he labeled the id, the ego and the super-ego. The new born infant is completely id-dominated. It behaves as it wants to without regard to its surroundings or the wishes of others. All of us, said Freud, would like to continue to act like this uninhabited baby. We would like to satisfy our feelings of aggression, sexuality and other impulses which would gratify our sensuous nature (libido). However, as the infant grows, he becomes socialized. He is made aware that he cannot act in an unrestrained manner and must learn control. Thus his ego is developed. This ego is the part of the being which is exposed to the other group members. This is the acting human being who has learned to control the id and thus cope with reality.

In most civilizations a third and very important element is added. This is the super-ego. In order to keep the ego from rebelling and satisfying the id, the super-ego acts as a check on our actions. We usually refer to it as our conscience. Thus if our super-ego has been well developed, and if we have been properly socialized, we will act in a rational manner even when we might be tempted to act more impulsively. This is indeed a major part of many religions. The Christian-Judaeo doctrine emphasizes that even when no man sees what we have done, God is ever present and knows our every move. In fact He even knows our thoughts and the orthodox believer should feel as guilty for immoral or indecent throughts as he would had he actually committed the forbidden act. The Bible is most emphatic about this for we read that the man who has adultorous thoughts is as guilty as the man who puts such thoughts into action.

Many psychologists and psychiatrists, while recognizing the monumental nature of Freud's work, disagree with some of his conclusions. They point out that Freud lived and worked in one type of culture in one period of history and that this influenced his findings especially in the area of sexual behavior. For example he concluded that there is a stage in human development in which the sex urge becomes latent and indeed his observation of his social environment might have seemed to uphold this belief. This period of latency was from about age 5 or 6 until the child experienced pupery. Various anthropologists, including

Margaret Mead, found that in certain primitive cultures there was no such period and that sexual activities were evident among the young during this supposedly latent period. Thus it could be concluded that in Europe which Freud knew, it only appeared that the sexual urge became latent. Whereas in actuality it was ever present but was rather effectively hidden due to the pressures imposed by the puritanical beliefs of late 19th Century and early 20th Century Europeans and Americans.

Other critics of Freud maintain that many of his findings are biased in that most of his work was with abnormal individuals who suffered from various degrees of mental illness.

In spite of these and other criticisms of Freud, there are none who would detract from the great pioneering and original work he performed in the field of human behavior.

One of the most interesting psychological theories of recent origin is that developed by Kurt Lewin which he called the Topological Field Theory. This theory is based on the life space view of our existence. The life space for an individual are those aspects of his environment which are relevant to his being. Within the life space various forces are always present. These forces may be compared to those in a magnetic field as they have plus or minus characteristics. Those which can be considered plus or positive are called driving forces in that they have a tendency to push a person toward a particular decision or act. At the same time there are negative or minus forces at work which are called restraining forces in that they have a tendency to prevent the person from taking a certain course of action. Lewin's theory is closely related to the concept of ambivalence, a characteristic which seems to be present in all human beings. We tend to look at certain people or situations with completely opposite simultaneous feelings. Freud maintained that most of us love and hate a person (husband, wife, father, mother, etc.) at the same time. He also believed that while all of us had the urge to survive, we also had a wish to die. Certainly ambivalence is evident in much of what we do. Saint Paul, writing in the New Testament, expressed it by saying that that which he should do he did not and that which he should not do he did. A song that was popular not too many years ago expressed the plight of the individual who didn't want to leave but also didn't want to stay. We often say that we have mixed feelings about a situation. Lewin would say that this is because the driving and restraining forces are affecting us. A good example might be the student who is confronted by the choice of studying for tomorrow's class or watching television. On the one hand he is aware of the importance of making a passing grade in the course. He knows that unless he studies, he will not be prepared and his grade will suffer. In the long term view his college work is more important than any television program. There probably are many additional factors which would dictate that he study. On the other hand there are forces which restrain him from doing his work. The program is one he has been looking forward to seeing. He is tired and feels that he should relax. He may rationalize that he already knows the assigned material even though he does not. In other words he must make a decision and there are forces which will affect that decision.

No matter how we view human motivation or which theory or theories we accept, we remain confronted with a most intriguing subject: It is probably safe to assume that all behavior is purposeful. Edward C. Tolman (1886-1969) in his study of motivation and learning concluded that behavior could not be explained entirely by stimulus-response, physiological or psychoanalytical theories because as he put it man possesses a "mentality" which introduces an infinite number of variables into the life of any human being.

From the human relations point of view it is not so important that we agree or disagree with the various theories which have been presented but rather that in our day to day association with others we recognize that we are all unique. We should, therefore, try to look behind the overt action and try to discover the reasons for the action. If we do this, we may better understand the reason for the specific behavior and it is for this goal that we should strive.

CHAPTER THREE

PERCEPTION, THE GREAT VARIABLE

"Strike three, you're out!" calls the umpire in his most authoritative voice.

"Out! You're blind! That was a ball!" explodes the batter with a look of disbelief on his face.

This little drama is repeated hundreds of times across our nation during the baseball season and illustrates a very basic characteristic of human beings called perception. In this situation we find two individuals supposedly well qualified in their assigned roles. Both are assumed to have good eyesight or else they would not be where they are. The ball is thrown by the pitcher. Both the batter and the umpire know that it is going to be thrown and are ready for it. The number of decisions required in this instance is extremely limited--the pitch can be either a ball or a strike. There is no other alternative. For all practical purposes both men observe the ball at about the same time. Both must make a judgment. Both do make this judgment but for some reason the results are completely opposite.

Perception has to do with our five senses--sight, hearing, taste, smell and touch. All stimuli reach our brain through one of these sensory routes. However, although several individuals may receive the same stimuli, differences in perception take place due to the fact that they all do not select, organize and interpret the data in the same manner. Judges, lawyers, police officer and others who are concerned with courtroom evidence are constantly aware of this. In case after case where honest and reliable citizens have been witnesses to the same accident, the variations in testimony are almost unbelievable. Classroom experiments have further reinforced the fact that perception of the same situation may vary significantly from person to person.

One of the prime examples of this matter of perception is in the tasting of food. What tastes delicious to one person may be unpalatable to another. It would seem that such a simple and obvious situation would have little or no bearing on human relations but in actuality such differences may be the basis of disharmony between husbands and wives, parents and children and friends. How many children have grown up with resentment toward the mother who forced them to eat a particular item which they actually despised? The tragedy in such cases is that the mother probably had the best of intentions but lacked the imagination or knowledge to either substitute another item or wait until the child reached a point of readiness in the acceptance of the particular food. Taste is indeed a matter of individual perception. How can we ever really know how food tastes to someone else? If the individual claims that the coffee is too strong (hot, sweet, bitter, cold, etc.) who are we to disagree with him. He is the one who is perceiving the coffee and he can only do this with his own sensory equipment.

The entire subject of perception is of tremendous importance in considering marriage and the family. When two people become man and wife, they should realize that they will not always see every situation in the same way as does the other. Often the differences in perception may be over a "trivial" matter. That is it is trivial in the eyes of one but not the other. One young couple almost reached the point of separation (or at least separate beds) because of a pillow. The wife preferred a large pillow and naturally felt that for the appearance of the bedroom both pillows on the double bed should be the same size. The husband, on the other hand, had always preferred a small pillow and found the large one most uncomfortable. Although he suggested that for appearances the two large pillows could be on the bed during the daytime, the wife felt that this was too much trouble and that it would be easier and better for him to sleep on the large pillow. Fortunately the problem was resolved when the wife finally accepted the husband's solution but it can be seen that a simple matter of perception can have possible serious repercussions.

It is obvious that because people are different, their perception is different. All of us do not have the same physical equipment. Further all of us do not develop our senses to the same degree. Theoretically the detective, the artist or the psychologist should be better observers than individuals in some other vocations. However, no two detectives, artists or psychologists will always see the same object, person or scene in the same way. Next we must consider the matter of memory. Some individuals can retain the results of the sensory stimuli longer and more completely than others. Finally, there is the matter of words. While two people may perceive a situation in the same manner, they may express their perception differently and thus precipitate a disagreement.

When we consider the problems involved in the perception of the physical world, the possibility of differences in the perception of the abstract aspects of life is infinitesimal. Our entire concept of right and wrong, moral standards or religious beliefs are related to our perception. To some people, divorce is tabu. To others divorce is not only permissable, but it is actually desirable in some cases. The current controversy concerning the legalization of abortions is another case in point.

On the more individual and person-to-person level, the behavior of others is largely a matter of how it is perceived.

The individual on the job may have the feeling that the boss is not pleased with his work. The boss has never mentioned this, but the worker feels that he might be in danger of loosing his job. Now he regards every move the boss makes in his presence and every word directed at him as a threat. When the supervisor casually asks him how things are going, he becomes even more apprehensive. Although the boss may be well satisfied with the man's performance and has no intention of dismissing him, this is not what the worker perceives.

In the physical world we can perhaps readily recognize that peoples' sensory systems differ and that they are not constant. The driver who is extremely tired or upset may not be able to drive as well as one who is rested. In the area of interpersonal relationships it is not always so easy to explain why perception varies. Part of the explanation will be discussed later terms of stereotyping and scapegoating. But there are some other considerations. It has been demonstrated that our perception of situations is strongly affected by our past experiences and environment. Dr. Joyce Brothers neatly made this point in a recent radio interview. She used the example of the husband who has just come from the market with some steaks. As the wife looks (perceives) at them, she asks, "Where did you get these steaks?" The husband immediately responds, "Why, what is wrong with them?" Now the wife in this case did not say by words or tone that there was anything wrong with them. In fact she wanted to say how good they looked but the husband perceived her remarks as unfavorable. Why? Could it be that as a child he was usually criticized and thus grew up to be on the defensive? Another example used by Dr. Brothers involves the husband asking the wife, "Where are my silver cuff links?" And the wife replies, "wherever you left them the last time you wore them." In all probability, according to Dr. Brothers, the wife makes this reply because this was the manner in which she was answered by her parents when she was a child. The point in both instances is that we tend to react in adult situations in much the same manner as we did when we were children. Or to make a broader statement, our perception of the present is the result of our past experiences and environment as well as the environment in which we find ourselves now. Of course, if this is true, it would dictate that parents should be extremely careful in the manner in which they respond to their children's needs. More important for us who have already reached adulthood, it is of vital importance that we try to remember that the person with whom we are dealing is the product of his past just as we are of ours. If we can adhere to this attitude, we may avoid many of the problems which arise so easily due to faulty perception.

Although perception is an individual matter, there are certain results of faulty perception which have a tremendous impact on our lives as individuals and as members of groups. The first of these is the tendency of people to perceive others in what is referred to as a stereotype. The adoption of this word as a psychological term is significant. Originally stereotyping referred to a process used in printing by which a metal plate was cast by the use of a matrix (mold) made of some other materials such as paper-mache. Once the mold was cast and the plate was produced, the letters, pictures, or other features were in permanent form until the plate was broken or melted for reuse. The stereotype was the fixed and rigid representation of the material to be printed.

In the psychological sense, the stereotype is formed in our minds. It is a preconceived notion of how people of another race, religion, national origin, socio-economic level or occupation ought to behave. The person who classifies all Germans as unimaginative and scientific is stereotyping. People often develop stereotypes after little or no contact with the people being judged. Thus the country child who is brought up to believe that all people who live in cities are "dishonest" will have this opinion even though he may not have had any contact with city dwellers. One of the authors knew a college president who exemplified this despite the fact that he was an extremely well educated and intelligent man. At one time the head of the Reserve Officers Training (ROTC) program at the college was a native of New York City. This man, an Army Colonel, did not perform his duties in the manner expected by the president. The president finally asked the Army to replace the colonel with someone else. He specified that the replacement must be someone who was raised in a small town or in the country. Over the years as various ROTC department heads served at the university, the president continued to specify that he would not accept anyone from a large city as if there were a relationship between the individual's place of birth and his efficiency as a member of the college staff.

The sequel to this incident is rather ironic. Many years later when it was time for a new officer to be assigned as the head of the ROTC program, the man designated by the Army happened to be a native of New York City. The president contacted the Army headquarters and stated that he would prefer someone who was not from a large city. After some discussion concerning the outstanding qualities of the man under consideration, the president relented and decided to accept him. Within less than a year it was apparent that the colonel did not meet the standards desired by the president. Again he contacted the Army headquarters and asked that the colonel be relieved and that a new man be assigned. The Army complied with his request. The president was more convinced than ever that his impression of the Army officers who had been raised in large cities was correct. Of course, we will never know how much the president's perception of the colonel influenced his decision to have him replaced. Could it be that the colonel was actually doing a good job but that the president perceived it otherwise because of the strong stereotype he had formed? Or could it be that the colonel's performance was affected by his knowledge that the president had an unfavorable opinion of city people? We do not know all the answers to this situation but it does provide us with a classic example of stereotyping and it illustrates the point that all of us are subject to forming judgments based on falacious reasoning.

Recently some news items have appeared which have brought attention to the problem of stereotyping. In one release Jerry West, the great Los Angeles Lakers professional basketball star, commented on his nick name, "Zeke." West is a native of Cabin Creek, West Virginia and some of his associates began calling him "Zeke from Cabin Creek." "I don't like it" said West. "It sounds like a put down. It makes it sound as if all the people where I come from are dumb or stupid. That's just not true. They're good -- just as smart and nice as anybody else."[5] To West the nickname "Zeke" stereotyped the people from his native region. One might ask why a person would become upset over the use of a name. After all Zeke can be used as a proper name and is actually a shortened form of the honored Biblical name of Ezekial. If West knows that the people from his home town are as good and smart and nice as anyone else, why should he resent being called Zeke? After all the name is merely four letters arranged in a certain order. It is difficult to rationally analyze such reactions. All we know is that the person does object to the name and that is sufficient to cause a real human relations problem.

On the wider and more dangerous level we can illustrate the point by the use of words such as nigger, wop, kike, spic or other terms which have been applied to certain ethnic groups. Why should a person take offense (often violent) to a series of letters? It is apparent that these letters when placed in a set order and applied to a given group or individual have an emotional content which defies rational explanation. Few people seem to believe the wisdom of the childhood jingle that "sticks and stones will break my bones but names will never hurt me." Names apparently do hurt people to such an extent that wars have been fought, riots started and people murdered because of a word which was used in conjunction with stereotyping.

An interesting aspect of this phenomenon is found in the story of comedian Bill Dana. Bill created a fictitious character called Jose Jiminez. Jose was an appealing and amusing Mexican who had all sorts of misadventures. Recently Mr. Dana announced to a group of Mexican-Americans that he had decided to end forever the role of Jose.[6] In fact he stated that Jose was dead and to emphasize this fact he publically read his obituary. According to Dana some Mexican-Americans complained that the characterization of Jose reflected adversely on them and gave the impression (stereotype) that all Mexicans were slow, lazy, stupid, uncoordinated and blundering. Although Dana stated that he had never intended for this to be the case, and indeed did not regard Jose in this light, he would never again portray the role. This was a major decision on the part of Dana when it is considered that his creation of this comic character made him famous and brought him large amounts of money. Later Mr. Dana further explained his decision to "bury" Jose. "There was no pressure. My friends from Mexico loved Jose. They said what are we if we have no sense of humor about ourselves? But it was people from this country who would tell me, 'Boy I sure love it when you play that dumb Mexican.' That made me drop the character. To people like that any Latin is a dumb Mexican." Thus we can see that the existence of the stereotype was instrumental in Mr. Dana's decision.

In a similar trend we have seen in recent years the decline of the number of ethnic anecdotes which were once so popular. Many people now feel that it is not proper to tell jokes involving lazy Negroes, cheap Scotchmen, drunken Irishmen, hot tempered Italians and scheming Jews.

Not all stereotyping takes place with respect to particular races, religions or national origins. The mere appearance of an individual is enought to bring about the stereotype. This has been especially true since the "hippie" movement began in our society a few years ago. This is well summarized by this quotation from a recent news story. "Wear your hair long, don blue jeans, hang a trinket around your neck, and automatically you alienate most people -- especially parents, employers, shopkeepers, policemen, and school authorities." Many older generation Americans judge an individual by his clothes, his hair length or whether or not he has a beard. The stereotype here is that all young men with long hair and/or a beard are dirty, perverted, disrespectful and probably drug users. On the other hand the so-called clean cut boy in the well fitting suit with a neat hair cut and close shave is thought to be honest, clean, respectable and completely normal. As is so often the case with people who use stereotyping the judgments are made after little or no contact with the group being judged. In actual fact the boy with the "hippie" appearance may be of high moral character, completely honest and most respectful to his elders. On the other hand the young man in the so-called "straight " garb may be unreliable, morally degenerate and completely dishonest. In fact most "con" men who live by defrauding unsuspecting individuals make it a point to give the appearance of respectability by wearing acceptable clothing and grooming themselves in the most acceptable manner. It must be made clear that many individuals who fall into the "hippie" category meet the stereotype judgment of the observer, but many of them do not. The point is that when we judge people on outward appearances we are in danger of letting the stereotype take the place of rational judgment.

A recent Harris Survey emphasized the danger that is inherent in stereotyping.[7] This national survey showed that "one of the ironies of American's racial agonies is that the less contact white people have with blacks, the more they tend to fear racial

33

violence." Conversely white people who know and have frequent contact with blacks are less worried about the outbreak of such violence. Herein may be the answer to the problem of stereotyping. We know that people can change their attitudes and their preconceived notions about other groups under certain conditions. One of the most dramatic examples of this can be found in the many incidents where white and black soldiers have served in combat together and saved each others lives. However, all of us are not going to have such dramatic experiences. Many authorities believe that the eventual complete integration of the schools will be the biggest step in the elimination of the black-white stereotype. Just as the American melting pot has in time boiled away the attitudes which stereotyped all Irish, Germans, or Scandanavians, so in time the same process may change the racial situation. Of course, this is the view of one group. At the same time another group maintains that the black-white stereotype is correct and that it will continue to persist. In any event from a psychological viewpoint it would appear that more contact with the groups involved plus strong educational efforts are probably the only methods by which any progress can be made in this most vital area.

Closely related to the development of stereotypes is the development of perceptual sets. It is to be regretted that although human beings have much in common, they seem to focus on the differences which exist. This, of course, results in antagonisms and human relations problems of varying degrees of seriousness. As we grow and are exposed to a particular type of training and environment we develop attitudes, values and predispositions which are often more emotional than they are rational. These become part of our personality and character and become deeply rooted in our make up. They are called sets.

An example of a set is the halo effect which is closely related to stereotyping but is less extensive in scope and usually applies to a specific individual. In the case of the halo effect the individual who uses it does so after some contact with another person. It can be described as the act of making a favorable judgment based on a limited and often irrelevant observation. It is evident in many aspects of our daily lives. The interview situation is a good example. The executive needs to hire a typist and several girls apply for the job. One of the girls is by far the most intelligent and most capable typist but she is slightly overweight and her clothes are not as stylish as they might be. Another girl is mediocre in her typing ability and is not too smart, however, she is very attractive and dresses well. The executive hires her. It may be argued that the attractive girl will be more of an asset to his office, but if he is looking for brains and the ability to type, he hired the wrong person. Of course, this is one reason why business teachers instruct their students in personal grooming as an aid in obtaining employment.

Another common example of the halo effect takes place in any organization when people are being considered for promotion. In the group under consideration for advancement to the next higher position is an individual who at one time made a very favorable impression on the boss because of one act which he had performed. Since then he has not been outstanding but the memory of that one act remains in the mind of the supervisor. To put it another way, every time the boss looks at this individual, he figuratively sees a halo (the favorable act) around his head. This person now receives the promotion even though others in the group may be more qualified than he is. Military organizations have been prone to use the halo effect. Many an old soldier received repeated promotions because of some meritorious act performed in the past. It could be said that he is "living" (resting might be a better word) on his laurels.

There is no field of human endeavor which is immune to the halo effect. Education is certainly no exception. The time worn phrase, "teacher's pet" is an expression of the fact that for some reason the favored pupil can do no wrong in the sight of the instructor and thus receives favored treatment.

The halo effect can work in reverse and be as unfair as the instances referred to above. Again we can use a group of workers to illustrate the point. On one occasion one of them incurs the displeasure of the boss because of his failure in a specific task. Although the failure was not serious and although the individual has more than made up for it since, to the boss it continues to exist and that individual may be finished as far as further advancement is concerned. Perhaps instead of the term "reverse halo" we might better describe this as "the albatross effect" for just as the ancient mariner was doomed to carry the symbol of his one foolish act around his neck forever, so might the individual be forced to live with one penalizing incident from his past. The young football player who ran the wrong way in the Rose Bowl game many years ago never lived down his error. Despite the fact that he was and continued to be an outstanding player, his positive accomplishments were forgotten as the press and the public remembered him as the wrong way runner.

Human beings want to be right. Henry Clay, one of the great American statesmen probably expressed this as emphatically as possible. Mr. Clay had a burning ambition to be President of the United States and there were many who thought that he could fulfill this desire. However, in 1850 he publically defended the provisions of the Missouri Compromise. When one of his advisors told him that this poisition would seriously endanger his chances of ever being President, he made the often quoted reply, "Sir, I would rather be right than be President." Such a position is admirable and there is certainly nothing wrong with wanting to be right. However, as is often the case with people, their personal desires and their opinion of themselves affects others with whom they are in contact. Because of this we can observe what is referred to as the "self-fulfilling" prophesy. This phenomenon occurs when we expect responses to take place and because of our expectations they in fact do. Our "predictions" come true. This can be illustrated in many ways and examples are to be found in every area of our lives. A man and his wife are invited to attend a social affair and they feel that they must go. The wife is looking forward to the event as one which will be enjoyable. The husband, on the other hand, does not want to go and repeatedly tells his wife that he is not going to enjoy himself. They attend and the husband's self prophesy is fulfilled. He does not enjoy himself at all and continues to grumble about the situation all the way home.

Parents often reveal this in dealing with their children. The parent who refuses to trust the child will probably find that the child does become untrustworthy. If the child is accused of lying often enough, he will in all probability lie. One of the writers once interviewed a 14 year old boy who had been a disciplinary problem to all of his teachers. When he was asked for an explanation of his behavior, he replied quite frankly, "What do you expect of me? I'm in the dummy group." He was right. Every one of his teachers expected him to perform poorly academically and from a behavioral point of view. He did not disappoint them. Unfortunately the self-fulfilling prophesy seems to be quite prevalent in school situations. Rosenthal & Jacobsen in their book, *Pygmalion in the Classroom*, present this analysis.

"Entering the first grade classroom is a big step for a child. It can be a glowing or a devastating experience. The teacher smiles at the children, looking at them to see what the year will bring. The well groomed white boys and girls will probably do well. The black and brown skinned ones are lower class and will have learning problems unless they look exceptionally clean. All the whites who do not look tidy and need handkerchiefs will have trouble. If the teacher sees a preponderance of lower class children, she knows her work will be difficult and unsatfying. The teacher wants her children to learn, all of them, but she knows that middle class children do do well. All this she knows as she smiles at her class for the first time, welcoming them to the adventure of the first grade, measuring them for success or failure against the yardstick of middle classness." At the end of th year the grades on the report cards and the comments concerning deportment will show that the teacher had been an accurate prophet. She could not fail to be. She not only made the prophesy, but also insured that it would be correct.

Most people are guilty at times of using the devices discussed in this chapter, thus it is extremely important that we recognize that they do exist and are part of our pattern of behavior. It is only when we are aware of them in ourselves and in others that we can begin to modify our behavior in such a way that they will be positively modified or completely eliminated.

It might be discouraging to realize that humans are prone to stereotype, use the halo effect and indulge in the self fulfilling type of prophesy. If these are as prevalent as they seem to be and if we develop perceptual sets, what hope is there for the improvement of our human relations? Taking a pessimistic viewpoint we might decide that there is little hope and that man's inhumanity to man is evidence of this. We ask ourselves why one nation wars on another. We ask why one group persecutes another. Intellectually we decry discrimination, hatred and war. But how can we expect nations, religious groups, racial groups and other such entities to exist in harmony when we find husband against wife, father against son, brother against brother, neighbor against neighbor and friend against friend? We can easily loose hope and proclaim that there is little chance of any improvement in the behavior of human beings.

On the other hand, there is the more optimistic point of view. John Ruskin said that "Education is not teaching people what they do not now know, but rather it is teaching them to behave in a manner in which they do not now behave." If this is true, and we like to think that it is, then there is hope. If in all our attempts to educate we would keep behavioral change as our objective, we could accomplish much in improving man's relationship with other men. Sets, no matter how deeply they may be engraved in the mind of an individual can be changed. Not in every case perhaps and not easily, but it can be done. There are many individuals in our nation today who have changed sets which they had held for many years. There are people who violently opposed the concept of the Federal Government entering into areas which at one time were considered purely local matters, but today they accept the fact that in some cases such intervention is essential. In the field of race relations which we shall look at in more detail in a later chapter we also see that many individuals in our country have changed their attitudes and beliefs in this very sensitive area of human relations. It is not uncommon for college students to make the comment that their parents are racially prejudiced and that they were also but as they have become more familiar with members of the other race, they have gained a new understanding and have lost some, if not all of their former feelings. In the field of religion, another very tradition conscious area of human activity, we see attitudes changing.

It is essential that we adopt the view that not only are sets subject to change, but such change is imperative for the survival of mankind. This, of course, is the goal in human relations activities.

CHAPTER FOUR

SOME MECHANISMS OF THE MIND

The human brain is probably the most complex organ in our body. Although we can describe its size, shape and structure and although we have isolated various areas and determined their specific function, the workings of the brain remain a mystery beyond man's present comprehension.

In this chapter we will examine and discuss various mental processes which human beings use under certain conditions. The processes are called defense mechanisms. For a better understanding of one's own thoughts and actions and those of other people, it is important that we have some knowledge of these devices of our brain which we all use to some extent.

It can be said without reservation that all of us living in twentieth century America face frustrations from time to time. Even the individual with the best adjustment to his environment will be confronted by situations which disturb the course of his existence. These frustrations may be extremely trival or they may be gigantic in scope. In any case, once we are in the frustrating situation, we try consciously or subconsciously to escape. Sometimes this can be accomplished by physically leaving the area, but this may not always be possible or desirable. In some cases we may decide to forget our frustrations by resorting to alcohol or drugs. This we know is far from being a recommended solution although modern medicine has made great use of the tranquilizing drugs to assist individuals in lessening their tensions. The extreme act of escape is that of suicide and unfortunately this has become all too prevalent in our world today.

Fortunately, most people do not resort to such extreme methods but choose those which are more subtle. These are called <u>aggressive reactions</u>, <u>withdrawal reactions</u>, and <u>compromise reactions</u>. For our purposes we will not discuss all of the mechanisms in each of these categories but will describe those which seem to be the most relevant to problems in human relations.

As the term implies, the aggressive reactions are those by which the frustrated individual takes the offensive. He is in a situation which is uncomfortable and he is going to try to do something about it. One of the most common devices is known as <u>scapegoating</u>. Here the individual seeks some other person or group of persons on which to vent his frustration. The school teacher who may be having marital problems is able to "take it out" on her students by threating them in a harsh and even unjust manner. On the other hand, the teacher who is frustrated by her students may display her temper and frustration in her relations with her family when she arrives home. Scapegoating can also take place on a large scale. This was quite evident in Germany prior to World War II when Hitler declared that the Jews were responsible for the economic problems of the nation. Marx, by placing the blame for the world's ills on the capitalistic class, was also using scapegoating.

Closely related to scapegoating, but different, is the mechanism known as <u>free floating anger</u>. Here the individual does not select a particular scapegoat but exhibits his anger in a general way. We often describe such people as "being mad at the world." These individuals seem to be hostile in almost every situation with little or no apparent cause. These are the individuals who can become extremely angry over what would be considered by most as a minor frustration. However, we cannot make that judgment. What might appear to be insignificant to one person may be very large in the mind of another.

Of course, both scapegoating and free floating anger can be dangerous. The persecution of the Jews in Germany (and in many other countries) is proof of this. We also know that the individual who exhibits feelings of free floating anger, may eventually display this anger physically by attacking the person or persons who displease him.

<u>Withdrawal reactions</u> may take the form of actual physical withdrawal or of a withdrawal by the mind only. Probably the most common form of this latter method is the use of <u>fantasy</u> or "day dreaming." Who of us has not been in a boring classroom completely frustrated by the limitations which have been placed on us? We cannot leave the room as this is where we are scheduled to be at this time. No matter how hard we try, we just cannot become interested in the lecture. A similar situation might, and does, take place on a warm Sunday morning when the sermon is long and the pews are hard. Again we are trapped, but there is escape through the use of the mind if not the body. It is not difficult in these situations to picture ourselves engaged in some more appealing activity somewhere else. We can escape to such an extent that we may completely forget where we are. There is evidence that even at a very young age human beings have this capacity. Such behavior appears to be normal and useful, however, a word or two of caution. If while we are engaged in this fantasy, the teacher covers test material, we may find ourselves wishing that we had not taken flight on the wings of our imagination. There is a more serious danger than just the possibility of failing an exam. The person who constantly resorts to fantasy might be heading toward mental illness. When the individual reaches the point where the fantasy is reality, we know that he has crossed the line between being mentally healthy and mentally ill. Fortunately, most of us resort to the use of fantasy and recognize it as just that, a useful and harmless means of escaping frustration.

Often human beings say and do things which become a source of embarrassment, shame and guilt. Once done the act or words cannot be recalled. They are present in the conscious thoughts of the person and are a source of frustration to him. He would like to wipe out the incident but this is not possible, but wait, perhaps it is possible for this to happen through the mechanism called repression. This is not the same as forgetting but it is similar to a degree. Somehow the unpleasant memory of the incident is blocked out of consciousness. This is usually a complete process in that the individual will not recognize the existence of the repressed thought even if it is brought to his attention. It is important to note that although the thought has been pushed underground so to speak, it is still present and in fact may be a source of trouble to the individual. Often in psychotherapy the therapist is able to cause the person to release the repressed thought. Sometimes this is accomplished through the use of drugs or hypnotism. In some cases the psychiatrist can elicit the memory of the thought without resorting to these methods. Again we must look at the manner in which repression might affect a person. Much depends on the thought involved and how much it means to the individual. In some cases there are no ill effects while in others there may be.

Another form of evading unpleasant thoughts is through the use of suppression. This is the conscious decision not to think about something at that particular time. In "Gone with the Wind" Scarlet usefully practiced suppression when she made up her mind not to think of a particular problem "until tomorrow." Suppression is putting off the frustrating thought. The delay may be in terms of minutes, hours, days or any other periods of time. Here again the use of suppression can be most useful or it can be a disadvantage. The harried business man who is not able to suppress his throublesome thoughts but carries them from the office to his home may be a candidate for any number of disorders. If he tosses and turns all night because of the presence of the thought he certainly has a problem. How much better it would be if he could say to himself, "I'm going to leave that problem at the office and take care of it tomorrow." This does not mean that he does not make plans to solve whatever is bothering him, but it does show a more sensible approach to the situation. We all need to be able to put off worrisome thoughts until such time as they can be acted upon in a constructive manner. On the other hand the individual who never faces up to a problem and keeps evading it may also find himself in difficulty. As in so many other aspects of living, it is important to strike the happy balance.

Regression is another withdrawal reaction. This is easily recognized and most of us have utilized it at one time or another. To regress means to go back. In this case we are again in a frustrating situation so we act as we would have in a former period of our life, usually childhood. The husband who becomes upset with his wife, picks up a plate and breaks it on the floor. As a child if he had committed such an act, he would have probably been spanked, but as an adult he will probably escape such punishment. Of course, his wife may find some other way to discipline him, but this is not the point. The fact is that he has behaved like a child. Adults who pout, display unreasonable temper and become tearful with little or no provocation may also be regressing. It is interesting to note that children use the mechanism of regression in certain circumstances. Children who have passed out of the toddler stage and no longer speak "baby talk" may do so on occasion. This is seen frequently where a new baby is present in the family and the older brother or sister seeks attention by reverting to a former type of speech and action.

Is regression a harmful practice? Again it depends on the frequency and the intensity of the act. Just as the golfer who misses a crucial shot may toss his club and then feel better, so other such acts may serve to release tensions in a relatively harmless manner. On the other hand, if the acts of regression are frequent and uncontrollable, trouble can be ahead.

So much for some of the withdrawal reactions. Now we will look at defense mechanisms in the category of compromise reactions. Probably the most common in this area is rationalization. This is a means whereby we use our intellect to make excuses for ourselves. It is amazing what human beings will do to justify their actions. In rationalization we devise logical explanations (expressed or not expressed) for a situation which would otherwise result in our loss of approval or self esteem. The classic example of this is the story of the fox and the sour grapes. After many efforts to reach a beautiful bunch of grapes the fox finally had to give up. However, to cover his failure he made the remark that the grapes were probably sour anyway. A young girl entered a beauty contest intent on being the winner. She tried her best but did not even reach the final round of the contest. Although deeply disappointed, she told her friends that she didn't care and hadn't really tried to do her best because if she had won she would have had to have given up a year of her schooling. Students with poor report cards seem to be especially adept at rationalizing the reasons for their failure. The teacher was unfair. The teacher didn't like the way he wore his hair. The test was not clear. No one else in the class did well. In other words the student can manufacture numerous excuses which seem reasonable but he will not admit that he failed because he had not studied, had not turned in a required term project and had skipped many class sessions. It is probably safe to say that at some time or another we all resort to rationalization. This seems to be a normal activity among human beings. Again, however, if the individual rationalizes every failure or frustration, he will soon be recognized by his contemporaries as someone who will not face reality or admit that he may have some weaknesses.

The mechanism of __projection__ is also evident in our daily lives. The individual ascribes to others an undesirable trait which he himself possesses. The chronic liar accuses others of lying. The jealous wife claims that her husband is the jealous one. The cheat accuses others of cheating. The major characteristic of this mechanism is that the individual seems to justify his own actions by projecting them on to others.

__Sublimation__ is an interesting and often useful mechanism used by human beings who find their desires blocked. In this case the person is not able to perform the act or accomplish the desired feat. He then finds (either consciously or subconsciously) some socially acceptable act which will relieve his frustration at least to some extent. Freudians claim that sublimation is basically a means of sexual release. For example, a man and wife may be having marital problems related to their sex life. They may feel that they would be justified in divorce or in having an affair with some one else or even expressing their feelings violently. However, due to their background, character, moral code or religious convictions they find these solutions unacceptable. The man may become extremely active in civic affairs and devote all his spare time to them. He may be considered a leading citizen in the community and receive the acclaim of his associates. He has sublimated his sexual frustration in a socially acceptable way. His wife on the other hand might spend most of her time on the golf course where she becomes an outstanding player. Her name and picture is in the paper and she feels a sense of accomplishment. While all this is happening the sexual problem remains. However, both have used the device of sublimation as a substitute for the basic need. Many authorities claim that some of the most productive individuals in the world of art, sports, business and government become successful due to the sublimation of their frustrations.

Although the foregoing example is in the Freudian tradition others could be given in which the sexual factor would be difficult to identify. A young man works for an extremely domineering and autocratic boss. Because this young man is married and has a family to support he feels that he cannot leave his position at this time. Day after day he is exposed to the tyranny of his supervisor. He dreads every minute of the working day. He would like nothing better than to walk up to the boss, punch him in the nose and tell him what he could do with the job. Instead, he must keep working and saying, "yes sir" and "no sir." What does the young man do about this situation? Nothing consciously but recently he became interested in karate. Now he spends two evenings a week at the karate club. Here he engages in vigorous and stimulating physical activity. He says it relieves the pressures of his job and it probably does. Even though he still detests his boss, he finds it easier to stand him since he has become engaged in his new found hobby which helps him give vent to his feelings. It should be apparent that sublimation is a healthy and useful device. Of course, we would prefer that the person not be in a position where he would have to sublimate, but at some time or another many of us have to use this mechanism.

An interesting commentary involving the organized use of sublimation has been reported from Japan. Since World War II, that nation has become so highly industrialized that many of the traditional patterns of life have dissappeared. The Ministry of Labor has found that with the advent of assembly lines and related features of big industry, there has been a "rapidly increasing number of tensions, irritations, frustrations, emotional and mental disturbances among workers." Recongizing this, the hugh Matsushta Electric Company has instituted a program which makes use of the sublimation technique plus other means by which workers can release some of their feelings in socially acceptable ways. A "selfcontrol" room has been established. Near the entrance to the room is a set of concave and convex mirrors to "give the worker a laugh at seeing his own distorted image. Next there is a small gymnasium, where the worker can start getting rid of pent-up tensions by punching bags, pedalling bikes and other exercise." Most unique is the next phase of this program. In a separate room "two life size padded dummies are seated on a knee-high platform. Bamboo staves are provided and the worker can club, swat or slash at the dummies to his heart's content, picturing in his mind anyone he likes as the object of the blows." The Matsushta Company apparently has someone in the company management who is psychologically oriented. Of course, Freudians would probably be able to make a case for a sexual explanation of the sublimating methods used.

Dr. Morton Golden, a Brooklyn psychoanalyst, has presented an interesting interpretation of the great popularity which football has gained through the media of television. Golden theorizes that men who spend long hours watching football may actually be sublimating their sex drives. "Men identify with the plunging halfback, the swashbuckling tacker, the crushing blocker, and eventually the athlete who scores." He believes that most men have a need to think of themselves as aggressive football heroes and that the games are used as a fantasy to relieve that "youthful sexual aggressiveness that may have ebbed with age and boredom." He further contends that the man who spends hours watching this controlled violence is in the same category as the woman who compulsively watches the many "soap operas" which make up much of the daily TV programming. Both the man and the women may be sublimating. Note that these activities are both socially acceptable and are not overtly sexual in nature. Of course, the sublimation involved is not on the conscious level and it is certain that the many armchair quarterbacks and serial watchers would strenuously deny Dr. Golden's allegations.

It is interesting to note that the great American author William Faulkener, while not psychologically trained, made a similar point many years ago when he said that the automobile had replaced men's wives as the objects of their attention. Faulkner wrote that when the man was washing, rinsing and waxing his car, he was using it as a substitute sex object. Apparently Dr. Golden believes that television football and soap operas have taken their place as an important means of sublimation.

If Freud were alive today, he would probably support Dr. Golden's views as they are in the true Freudian tradition.

Substitution, is a device which might result in serious consequences. Here again we find a frustrated individual, but in this case the frustration usually has sexual origins. The young boy who is not able to express normal sexual desires through dating or the husband who is not able to find sexual satisfaction with his wife may resort to substitution. Here the desire for sex is not replaced by another type of activity as a sublimation, instead the new activities are sexual in nature and usually antisocial. The young boy takes pleasure in writing obscenities on the walls of restrooms and in other places. The husband begins making obscene phone calls to females picked at random from the phone book. Some psychologists claim that such crimes as arson and shoplifing may provide sexual gratification to sexually frustrated individuals. In any event, it can be seen that substitution is dangerous not only because of the consequences of being caught in illegal acts, but because of the fact that even if the acts are not crimes (such as drawing suggestive pictures) they may produce guilt feelings which may cause eventual mental problems.

The final mechanism in the category of compromise reactions is that of compensation. Here the individual tries to overcome a weakness or an undesirable feature by developing a desirable one. The late Billy Rose might be used as an example of this. Rose was undersized, considered himself unattractive and as a youth had feelings of inferiority about his poor economic status and the fact that he was a member of a minority group (Jewish). Young Billy devoted long hours to becoming an outstanding stenographer. He held many records both for shorthand and typing. His ability was so well developed that he was soon receiving much publicity in the New York papers. Subsequently he was hired by a wealthy investment broker who recognized in him not only the ability to take shorthand and type but many other admirable qualities. Under the guidance of the older man, Rose steadily advanced in the world of business and became a millionaire at a very young age. Later he became one of the world's leading show business personalities whose activities became part of the great American success story.

The world of athletics also provides examples of compensation. Larry Hinson, a promising young professional golfer has one arm which is shorter and smaller than the other. Another champion golfer, Ed Furgol, also has one arm which is several inches shorter than the other. In spite of these handicaps which might rule out any golf at all, these two men became top performers in their chosen field. It is obvious that compensation is a useful and healthy device. However, there is a fine line between compensation and <u>overcompensation</u>. Some might say that Billy Rose actually overcompensated for his real or imaginary shortcomings, but how can this be judged? Examples of overcompensation can be given and it can be seen that if the compensatory acts are carried too far, the results can be disastrous. The undersized boy who feels inferior because of his small stature may forsake any idea of achieving success in the activities in which most boys succeed to a degree such as athletics, dating, and other forms of socializing. This boy now assumes the role of "tough guy." Through force and the threat of force he begins to terrorize the neighborhood. To do this he may have to resort to the use of weapons. He may also gather about him other boys in the formation of a gang. Soon he may be leading this gang in criminal activities. He is exhibiting what has sometimes been referred to as the "small man" complex. Ceasar, Napoleon and Hitler are usually given as examples of the operation of this mechanism.

Throughout this section reference has been made to mental illness. Some psychiatrists and psychologists regard such illness as a form of escape from the frustrations of reality. Many years ago Dr. George Esterbrooks wrote a very perceptive article entitled "The Sanity of Insanity." In this he developed the idea that the mental patient had achieved that for which most of us are striving. In other words, the patient who thinks that he is God, is God as far as he is concerned. Although Dr. Esterbrooks wrote this article in a semi-serious manner, he did make the point which is probably valid that the mentally ill person has escaped from whatever was frustrating him at the time. Although later knowledge in the field of psychiatry seems to negate this to some degree (many mental patients are extremely unhappy in their illness) there may still be some validity to Esterbrooks' conclusions.

In any discussion of human behavior it is inevitable that the question of normality be considered. In our everyday conversation we frequently use the term "normal." We are prone to make judgments concerning the normality or abnormality of other people's actions. The concept of normality, like many others in the study of humans, is a difficult one to define. Normal may refer to the individual from a physical viewpoint or from the psychological. One might think that it would be easy to determine the physical normality or abnormality of any given individual. In some cases this is true. The person who is blind does not have normal vision. The person who has muscular dystrophy does not have the normal use of his muscles. On the other hand what of those individuals who do not have any such readily observable conditions. In former years, doctors, upon the completion of an examination of a patient, would indicate on the record that the patient was normal. This is not necessarily true today. In many cases the phrase "within normal limits" is used indicating that individuals can vary markedly in certain physical aspects and still be called normal. Roger J. Williams in his book, You Are Extraordinary, exphasizes this point by saying that "normal individuals are highly distinctive with respect to their stomachs, esophagi, hearts, blood vessels, bloods, thoracic ducts, livers, pelvic colons, sinuses, breathing patterns, muscles and their system of endocrine glands."

If individuals differ so greatly in their physical characteristics is it not understandable that they would differ even to a greater degree in their behavior and still be classified as normal. Williams recognizes this by saying that "it is in the area of thinking that human beings have their most distinctive gifts."

What then is normal in the field of behavior? Sociologists like to tell us that at some time in some place every form of behavior has been acceptable. This is known as the principal of relativism. A widow in the United States who had her husband's body burned and threw herself on the fire would certainly be considered abnormal. At certain times in certain parts of the world the widow who did not do this would be the abnormal one.

One of the problems we have in discussing normality is that we think in terms of categories. We try to devise labels which are absolute. We try to think about black and white disregarding the fact that grey exists. We should try to adopt the concept of "within normal limits." We must think of individual behavior as occurring along a continuum. There are times when the psychotic person who is abnormal mentally acts as normal as those individuals who are not mentally ill. On the other hand there are times when the mentally well person acts as abnormally as the psychotic. Thus in arriving at a judgment as to the normality of any individual, we must have some idea of what his usual behavior is like. Even this can be an unreliable indication because under certain conditions an individual may behave in a completely acceptable manner but have periods of marked abnormality. During these latter periods he may encounter or create serious problems.

Thus far we have not come to any conclusion as to how the term normal should be defined as it pertains to behavior. When Freud was asked about this he said that there are two things a normal mature person should be able to do -- love and work. Many definitions of normal contain in essence this thought. The normal person is able to carry on his day to day activities and function in a manner which is acceptable to the group in which he lives. He is also able to love and be loved. This may sound easy but it is far from that. It is merely a functional and general description of the meaning of normality.

Often the question is asked as to whether normal and average have the same meaning when applied to human behavior. The answer is that they do not. Again let us look at an example using the physical characteristics. If we have the weights of one hundred first grade students, it would be very easy to arrive at an average weight for the group. Would an individual who deviated from the exact average be abnormal with respect to weight. Obviously not. In terms of the physical, we can measure and average, but even this does not tell us about normality. If this is true with the physical, it should be apparent that it is infinitely more difficult and probably impossible to arrive at some sure method of determining behavioral normality. How can we measure behavior? We cannot assign numerical values to behavioral traits, average them and arrive at a figure which would give us an average behavior. Even if we could, this would not answer our question about normality. It is not uncommon to have trained psychologists and psychiatrists disagree as to whether or not an individual is normal. In court cases, we see psychiatrists evaluating an accused person and arriving at opposite conclusions as to his sanity, or his ability to tell right from wrong. The experts in the case might be qualified, sincere and objective, but arrive at different answers. If this is so, how can we expect the layman to be able to make a judgment concerning the normality of an individual?

From the human relations viewpoint, we should be aware that normality is an elusive concept and one which should be approached with caution. We should not be too hasty in our judgment of our relatives, friends and associates. All of us may to some extent be guilty of the judgment made by the husband in the old quaker story. He told his wife that he believed that everyone in the world was peculiar "except for me and thee." He then added "and sometimes I wonder about thee."

CHAPTER FIVE

CONFORMITY VS NONCONFORMITY

Man is a gregarious animal. This means that he habitually associates with other humans in groups just as other species of animals travel in herds or packs. Although one might point to the existence of hermits, recluses and other "loners," the fact remains that these are the infrequent exceptions. Most men live lives in which the company of other men seems to be essential to the fulfillment of life as a human being.

As man lives in groups he tends to conform to the roles, definitions, and expectations of the group. For example so-called "white collar" office workers take on a uniformity of dress, hair styling, mannerisms and other characteristics of other white collar workers. One large company, in selecting and training its sales and technical representatives, insists that they present a certain image to the public. Thus they are required to dress in accordance with company guide lines. It has been said that the FBI under the guidancy of J. Edgar Hoover has a similar policy concerning the image of its agents. Nurses are not only easily recognized by their crisp white uniforms, but also by certain characterisitcs which are part of the role of being a nurse. In short, most of us fall into a certain mold depending upon the group or groups to which we belong.

The fact that we all belong to several groups simultaneously also has its effects on our dress and behavior. While at work in the city, the man may be recognized as a member of the banking profession. His suit, shirt, tie, and general grooming are almost like a sign which proclaims his mode of work. Now, the same man is at home in the suburbs. On the weekend he enjoys spending his time with his boat. As we observe him now, he no longer has on the "uniform" of the banker. Now he is easily distinguishable as a business man whose hobby is boating. He now is wearing the type of clothes associated with this recreational activity. He, of course, would not think of wearing his boating clothes to the office even though they might be far more comfortable and certainly more colorful. The same comparison might be made of golfers, campers, square dancers, bowlers, house painters, brick layers, truck drivers or members of any other such group. In each case we find the members conforming to certain standards of dress and general behavior.

It is an interesting phenomenon that often we become so accustomed to seeing a person in his usual type dress that it is hard for us to recognize him in another situation. This phenomenon is evident among young children. Often the child in kindergarten or first grade has difficulty in recognizing his teacher out of the classroom situation. Adults too, experience this to varying degrees. Not long ago one of the writers was sitting in the grill of a golf club after a round of golf. A lady acquaintance came over to the table and a conversation began. Also at the table was another member of the college staff. He was in his golfing clothes. The lady stated that she had applied for a job at the college and had an appointment the next day with one of the directors. She was rather embarrassed when she suddenly realized that this particular director was sitting next to her at the table. What made this incident even more indicative of the rolls we play, was the fact that she knew the director and had spoken to him several times at the college. It was clear as we all concluded that she had not recognized him in other than his "director's" clothes.

Conformity is one of the characterisitcs of group life. Designers of ladies and mens clothing and automobile manufacturers are well aware of this trait of mankind. When the mini skirt was introduced, it did not take long for the American girl to adopt it as her style of dress. If the history of fashion trends is an indication, the time will come (it may be here already) when the hemline will start dropping and might even reach a point below the knee. At the moment there are many girls who might say that they would never wear such long dresses but when and if such a time comes, they will conform as easily as they have to the many other style changes. It is not just the ladies who conform in such matters. A look at men's ties and lapel widths is proof that the male is also a conformist. If a man in 1960 had worn a wide tie, he would have been considered not only old fashioned, but something of an odd ball. However, the wide ties returned to style and now the man with the narrow tie is out of step.

Even the moral conotation which clothes carry changes with the times and becomes a part of our conformity. In the early 1900's it was considered immodest for a women to expose her ankle beneath the skirt. Gradually ideas of modesty changed to the point where the mini and the bikini are a part of our way of life and are worn by ladies and girls whose character cannot be questioned. Someone wrote to Dr. Billy Graham not long ago and asked his opinion on ladies wearing slacks or other types of trousers. He replied that in his opinion there was nothing at all wrong with this under the right circumstances. He mentioned that his wife often wore slacks while doing her work around the house or walking in the neighborhood. Not only did the Reverend Graham describe them as practical, but, and this is important, that in many cases they were more modest than a skirt. This is an interesting commentary on our times and on the entire matter of conformity. Certainly Mr. Graham must be aware that at one time in the not too distant past for a women to be seen in slacks or any type of trousers was considered highly immodest. A similar situation exists with respect to hair styling and the use of cosmetics. Again within the memory of the writers any women who dyed (bleached) her hair and "painted" her face was considered to be not only immodest but actually immoral. Preachers preached about this from the pulput pointing out that it was one more sign of the moral decay of mankind. Today, on the other hand, most of the ladies in the congregations of our churches, including the preacher's wife and daughter, not only use make-up, but many of them tint or color their hair.

As group members we conform in other than those outward appearances such as dress. Members of the Junior Chamber of Commerce, the Elks, The American Legion, the Rotary Club and other groups fit a recognizable mold. Now it must be asked why do most of us conform to certain patterns of behavior? As has been mentioned, such conformity is expected by our peers, thus there is a certain amount of pressure placed on us. This pressure may be spoken or written or it may be neither. If the conformity is required as a result of laws, codes, constitutions or similar statutes, it is considered formal in nature. All of us conform to an extent because of such formalized pressures. In many cases if we fail to conform (obey the law) we may be assessed with a penalty which could be light, such as a small fine or might be as drastic as life imprisonment or death. If we fail to follow the by-laws of a club to which we belong, we might also be subject to a penalty. Informal pressures to conform are not written, but they may be just as severe as those which are. In some primitive groups a person who fails to observe tribal customs may be disowned by the group and banished from it. In some cases he can never again resume his status as a group member and it is not uncommon for such a person to seek death by his own hand or through being deprived of his livelihood and place in the group. Our religious faiths and denominations provide good examples of conformity and the penalities for failing to conform. The price of non-conformity to religious standards may mean excommunication from the church here on earth and/or punishment in the hereafter.

We can see that conformity is dictated either by formal or informal means. One may be as rigid as the other and none of us can escape from the need to conform to some extent in our daily lives. How did such a system of human relationships begin in the first place? Why does man insist on individual conformity to group standards? To answer this it must be remembered that basically man is interested in survival. Early man had to be primarily concerned with satisfying those urges or needs which would insure group perpetuation. Thus it was essential that all members of the group act in a manner which would achieve this group goal of continuing to live and of producing new offspring. Today we spend much of our time in pursuits other than those essential to survival but the need to survive still exists. Further we have set up groups which have other goals and we have found that if these goals are to be reached, the group must make a united effort in which there is not much room for diversity or non-conformity. Thus we can say that by conforming, we help insure that group objectives will be met. We can also say that by conforming the individual helps insure that his own personal needs are met as they are closely related to the needs of the group.

Because we belong to more than one group we often encounter a situation which causes conflict. The young man has been a member of a family group which has very high moral standards. He has been aware of these standards since early childhood and accepts them as being of value. He is also a member of a church group in which the same standards are taught. There is no conflict at all between the views of the two groups. The young man graduates from high school and leaves home to attend college. He now belongs to the college group. Within the college group he may belong to the fraternity group. He soon finds that the fraternity group standards are quite different from those of his family and his church. Excessive drinking, illicit sex and perhaps the smoking of marijuana are accepted as the norm by the other members of the fraternity. While these other members may or may not have come from a similar background as the boy in question, they have by now been exposed to the pressure of conforming in the new group. Now the young man has a choice to make. Should he retain his family-church standards of conformity or should he accept those of the group which is now closer to him? In either case he may experience some bitter soul searching. If he decides to reject the teachings under which he was raised and conform to the standards of the fraternity, he may find himself burdened with deep feelings of guilt both from the religious and the psychological point of view. If on the other hand, he retains the standards of home and church, he may find himself considered "different" by his fraternity brothers. All of us belong to several groups. In most cases we choose those which are compatable with our way of life. However, as has been illustrated, this is not always true.

A large problem with respect to conformity is one which has always existed and which is especially evident today throughout the world. This is the trend wherein we see large numbers of individuals (especially the young) who do not seem to want to conform to the standards of society as a whole. There are several alternatives for such individuals. They may decide to conform outwardly while remaining bitter and frustrated within. This can be seen in the individual who follows a certain pattern of apparent conformity but inwardly considers himself a rebel. Another course of action for the non-conformist is to withdraw from the group in the full sense of the word. These few individuals are the ones who become hermits or recluses or drifters (hoboes used to be the term to describe this type of person). A third method of expressing this lack of conformity is in the acceptance of some new form of ideology. This is apparent today in the many cults which have emerged across America. There is the drug cult, the sex cult, the flower children and others. The members of these cults have established their own groups or societies to which they pay their allegiance. They have openly refused to conform to the norms of the larger society and have set up their own norms. It is interesting to note that although these movements began as protests against society, conformity in the new group is just as rigid and perhaps even more so than it was in the former situation. In viewing thousands of young people at a rock festival it was obvious that they had departed from the norms of dress and behavior to which they had formerly conformed. It was also obvious that they had adopted modes of dress and behavior which they now considered normal and to which they readily conformed.

There is a final step which the individual who does not want to conform might take. He might try to change the established norms through the use of pursuasion, reason, or some other acceptable method. An example of this might be taken from the history of our country with respect to woman's rights. For generations women had accepted the fact that they were excluded from voting, holding office or taking certain jobs outside the home. The vast majority conformed to this pattern of existence. From time to time non-conformists would emerge and attempt to change the situation, however, it was not until the beginning of this century that women began to make a concerted effort to gain some of the rights previously reserved for men only. Eventually there was enough pressure to cause the Congress to propose an amendment to the Constitution giving women the right to vote and in 1920 this was ratified.

Today, many young people who have been thwarted in their efforts to effectively bring their ideas to officials in Washington have begun to change their tactics. Whereas they formerly presented themselves in disreputable clothing, long hair and beards, they are now dressing in what might be called the "straight" manner of the establishment. They now find that they can gain entree to the various offices and present their greviances to previously "unavailable" officials.

As we take a broad look at history we see that there have always been non-conformists. While some of these individuals were regarded as radicals, trouble makers and general nuisances, many of these by their failure to accept the established norms made tremendous contributions to the nation or the world. We have only to think of Galilieo, Columbus, Martin Luther King, Henry Ford, Einstein General Billy Mitchell and many others to see the truth of this statement. Lincoln was probably one of the greatest non-conformists of all times. Had he lived, the entire history of our nation might have been changed as he was not ready to conform to the general northern attitude toward the defeated southerners. In more modern times we should consider Franklin D. Roosevelt. He was condemned as a socialist for wanting to introduce measures designed to alleviate much of the economic suffering in our nation. Today we accept the reforms he instituted as most desirable and fitting to our way of life.

The world and the groups in the world need conformity to insure continuity and stability. At the same time there will always be a place for the non-conformist to inject degrees of adaptability, flexability and progress. Of course, the dilemma lies in the balance required. Where does conformity become a liability and non-conformity an asset? There is no clear answer to this question. The major lesson in the field of human relations, with reference to conformity is that we should carefully evaluate the non-conformist before we act to condemn him.

There is another concept which is closely related to conformity and which has had an important effect on man's relations with other men. Sociologists have labeled this concept - ethnocentrism. Groups tend to regard their ideas, customs, beliefs and their entire culture as being superior to that of other groups. Further, they often believe that their ways are "right" while the ways of others are "wrong." This is ethnocentrism. We in the United States think that it is rediculous for the English to drive on the left hand side of the street and they are just as convinced that we are the ones who are doing it wrong. Many Christians look upon the plural marriage permitted to members of the Moslem faith as being sinful, whereas the Moslems believe that having more than one wife is in complete accord with religious doctrine. On and on we could go. Groups develop norms and come to accept them as being best.

What can be said about ethnocentrism and its effects on man's behavior? As usual there are two conflicting points of view. For a group to survive and maintain its group identity, a certain amount of ethnocentrism seems to be essential. We may think of this in terms of nations. Each nation tries to instill in its citizens the idea of patriotism and loyalty. Thus the nation is able to achieve the unity which is necessary to the perpetuation of the group. This is sometimes called nationalism. The often quoted phrase "My country, right or wrong" expresses the extreme view of ethnocentrism. At the same time it can be seen that such an attitude can and does lead to serious conflict. In the long history of warfare and strife it is obvious that national pride has often been a factor. Nations will fight to preserve what they believe to be their rights as nations. People will fight to preserve their "way of life." The American Civil war is perhaps the most tragic example of the evils of extreme ethnocentrism. In this bloody war, thousands of peopel were killed, for a cause which they believed was right.

When we consider war as the extreme expression of ethnocentrism, we recognize it as a wasteful and cruel activity. We sometimes wonder how one group of supposedly civilized people can deliberately set out to slaughter another group of humans. However,.

when we stop to think of the force which ideas have, it is little wonder that people of different races, nationalities or religions wage war on each other. After all, within communities, neighborhoods and indeed even within families, we find people disagreeing, fighting and killing because they are not willing to recognize that the other person may be right and that they may be wrong.

Thus we can see that although ethnocentrism has a useful purpose in unifying a group, it can also be dangerous. Again, as in so many human relations concepts, we must be able to establish a point where we should be able to make use of the desirable features while avoiding those which are undesirable. We admit that this is a most difficult task but that is just one more reason for trying to change people's attitudes so that we as human beings might make progress in achieving harmony among all people.

CHAPTER SIX

WORDS, WORDS, WORDS

One of the most useful skills of man is speech. Almost at the moment of birth the vocal chords of the new born child are in use. As the child grows, it steadily progresses from basic sounds such as crying, cooing and babbling to the use of words and then the formulation of sentences. However, even before words, the child is able to communicate with his mother and others by the use of sounds, facial expressions and gestures. Animals also possess this ability to some degree. Witness the dog which is hungry and is able to communicate this to its master, or the cows which are ready to be milked. It is apparent that animals can also communicate with others of their kind. Man, however, is in a special category for he has not only developed a system of spoken language but he has learned how to preserve words in written form. Thus, in addition to instantaneous communication, man can capture information and transfer it across the bounds of time.

How did language begin? How does the child learn language? Why is it that humans in one part of the world develop a different language from those in another? Why didn't one universal language develop? Or perhaps more importantly, why doesn't man develop a universal language in an attempt to eliminate some of the many problems which arise because he cannot always understand those who speak in another tongue? The subject of words and language is a fascinating one and has been the subject of study for centuries without much success in answering all the questions which can be asked.

Words are one of the most important aspects in the study of human relations. It can be readily demonstrated that words, their use and misuse, are often the root of many of the misunderstandings which take place among human beings. This goes beyond the matter of name-calling, mentioned previously, which has resulted in so much trouble and violence in the history of man. The problem seems to be that although we use words in our day to day communication with others, we are not always interpreting the same words in the same way. For example, how much is "not much," how high is "very high," how far is "a long way," how many are "several?" One might say that such questions really do not make much difference but is this always true? A newly married couple had their first real misunderstanding because of this vagueness of common words. The young wife was going to cook her husband a steak for the first time in their married life. Wanting very much to please him, she asked him how he wanted it prepared. He replied that he would like it well done. When the wife brought the steak, he was obviously displeased with it. He did not have to say anything as the expression on his face spoke as clearly as words. When she asked him what was wrong, he told her something to the effect that when he said well done, he did not mean burned to a crisp. Of course, this did not make the wife very happy and she proceeded to tell him that as far as she was concerned that was the way a well done steak should look and taste. As is so often the case in marriage and in other situations, personal relationships become damaged because of a misunderstanding or a misinterpretation over the use of a word.

The foregoing incident also reveals another facet of the entire problem of communication among humans. Man not only has a complex and diversified means of speaking, but he combines words with expressions. Sometimes, as in the foregoing case, the expression and the words say the same thing such as "this isn't the way I wanted the steak." Often, however, the words say one thing and the expression says something else which might even be a completely opposite idea. The ardent football fan has been waiting weeks to see his two favorite teams play the championship game. The time has come and he and his wife have settled comfortable before the television set. The first quarter has just begun when there is a knock on the door. Not only is it some old friends from out of town, who care nothing about football, but they have their four children with them and obviously are prepared to stay for the afternoon. The host and hostess verbalize the correct and polite expressions. "Oh how glad we are to see you." "Gosh it was nice of you to drop by." These are the spoken words, but if the visitors were perceptive they would note that the tone of the words and the facial expressions (especially the husbands) lacked the ring of sincerity. In fact the visitors may detect this difference between what was said and what was meant and may even decide to cut their visit short.

Another example of the difficulty we face with words is that which involves listening. Not only do we misunderstand what the other person may mean by the words he uses, but many times we do not even _try_ to understand him. This can be illustrated by citing what happens during an argument between two or more people. Soon they are all talking at once and no one is listening to anyone else. Of course, this chaos leads to further confusion and hard feelings and nothing is settled. The same process can take place in friendly conversation. Two friends meet and begin talking. If we watch and listen closely we will see that neither is hearing a word the other one says. Each is more intent on what he is saying or on what he is planning to say when the other pauses. There is really little or no communication. Children whose ages are between two and one-half to seven engage in a phenomenon called duel monologue. The two little ones appear to be engaged in conversation with each other. However, upon investigation it will be seen that what each says has no relation to what the other is saying. Adults are amused at this and may describe it as cute not realizing that they do the same thing time and time again. If you can recall the last party you attended or if you will take note during the next one you attend, you will see how much of this takes place.

Another difficulty with words is found in the fact that although man can be very receptive to ideas if he so desires, he can shut them out of his mind quite easily. School teachers could cite many examples of this. Teachers, especially new ones, are often shocked to find upon questioning certain students that they do not have the remotest idea of what was said. This situation is not limited to the classroom. It can take place anywhere at anytime. In the motion picture, "Midnight Cowboy," one of the theme songs illustrated this point clearly. The young man in the movie did not enjoy his dishwashing job in a restaurant. His boss and others were constantly calling him and giving him orders. The song going through his mind had these lines, "Everybody's talking at me, I don't hear a word they're saying only the echos of my mind." He felt that people were not talking TO him or WITH him but AT him. There is a world of difference expressed by the word AT. As a result he had in effect tuned out the words and now listened only to the echoes of his mind. In other words, he was more involved in his own thoughts than in what others were saying.

Words can be another source of trouble with respect to the way in which they are pronounced or because of their use in a manner to which we are not accustomed. It is interesting to note that in most countries there is a difference in pronounciation and expression from one section to another. Not only is this true in a nation as large as ours, but it is equally true in those which are much smaller. England, France or Italy are good examples of this. People from one section have difficulty understanding those from another even though they are all speaking English, French or Italian. Again the question might be asked as to why these differences arose in the first place but our concern is the fact that they do exist and they do contribute to human problems between the people involved. As previously noted, humans are ethnocentric. They like to think that their way of life, manner of dress and speech not only are the best but are "correct." Others are regarded as strange or foreign and not as "good." In the United States many a marriage between individuals from different parts of the country has been weakened because the two partners were not able to accept the other's way of speaking. This became a source of ridicule which leads to disharmony.

Another problem with words is the fact that the same word can have so many different meanings. We are referring to common words which we use everyday. This is sometimes made more complicated because the meaning of words changes over periods of time. The word "queer" is a good example of this. Today this word is commonly used in reference to homosexuality, but as recently as the 1951 edition of Websters Collegiate Dictionary such a meaning is not listed. The fact that words can have different meanings is important because whereas the person who uses the word may intend it one way, it may be taken in another by the person concerned.

Again the word "queer" is a good example. An older person might use it to mean eccentric, whereas the listener may interpret it to mean homosexual. Many similar examples could be given. If a person is referred to as "unbelievable," do we mean that he is a liar or that he is an unusual, remarkable or outstanding individual? The manner in which it is intended and the manner in which it is accepted may lead to trouble.

Words can be misused by removing them from context. This seems to be a favorite practice among some politicans. Not only do they take their opponent's words out of context, but they accuse others of doing the same to them. During the campaign the candidate may make this statement, "I believe in priorities. If elected I will not support any new building programs until those in progress have been completed." His opponent, however, uses only a part of the statement and tells his listeners that the other candidate "will not support any new building programs." The Bible is often quoted out of context to support ones own point of view. Some people might argue that Jesus preached that we should give no though to such material needs as food, drink or clothing and indeed this thought can be found in the Sermon on the Mount (Matt. 6:31). However, one must read the Thirty-Third Verse to have the full context. Jesus did not say that food, drink and clothing were not to be given consideration. What he said was that "But seek ye first th kingdom of God and his righteousness: and all these things (materia needs) will be added unto you." Too often we use only those parts of another person's words which are of use to us. We do not always tell all of the story.

Man is fortunate to have the use of a written and spoken language. At the same time he is bound by words to such an extent that he finds himself with problems. Our goal should be to make sure that we not only listen to the other person, but that we really understand what he is saying. At the same time we should make sure that our words, both written and spoken, leave little room for misinterpretation. Above all we should never lose sight of the fact that people do not always say what they mean nor do they always mean what they say.

CHAPTER SEVEN

SOME ASPECTS OF CHANGE

Perhaps it is unnecessary to say that change is inevitable. However, it is from this point that we must start to contemplate the importance of change in the lives of individuals and groups. Although we may find that certain institutions are relatively stable, most are in continuous state of development and reorganization. As times change, the groups in which we live must change to meet new situations. The Roman Catholic Church is usually regarded as extremely stable. However, even this great agency of conservatism has undergone major changes in recent years and more are being considered. The traditional Latin mass may now be celebrated in the language of the country. Certain dietary laws are no longer considered as important as formerly. The status of priests and nuns has been altered. This is even reflected in the modernization of the dress which many of the sisters may now wear. There has even been a change in the position which certain saints have long occupied in the hierarchy of the church. In other religions, changes in fundamental attitudes and beliefs have been made. This example of changes in religious institutions is used to point out that any organization or group, including those which are usually considered almost unchanging, are subject to change. This does not mean that all of the changes are accepted by all of the members. In fact many Roman Catholics have resisted some of the changes which they regard as too radical. However, the fact remains that the changes did take place.

One of the most quoted sayings concerning the subject of change is that "everybody resists change." This is not a true statement. In the first place we cannot make such an all inclusive statement about what "everybody" does or believes. We have to realize that individual differences and the manner in which individuals perceive an event are such that generalizations of this type seldom withstand close analysis. While it is true that many people resist change, it is just as true that many people welcome change. Certainly the person who is caught up in an almost hopeless environment would look forward to any change that would improve his situation, and even in this case there might be some who would prefer to remain in the known situation rather than move into the unknown. On the other hand the person who is comfortable in his status, including his job, his marriage, his neighborhood and his other interpersonal relationships might indeed resist change, but not necessarily.

The type of change and the manner in which it is made will influence the manner in which it is accepted by the persons concerned. Let us look at some concepts which might lead to a better understanding of change and the manner in which it can be introduced to individuals and groups.

Much depends on the person who is to initiate the change. If he has gained the prior confidence of the individuals concerned, it may well be that they will respond favorably based on the trust which he has established.

Another factor is the manner in which the individuals have been prepared for the change. If the leader or leaders see the need for change, they should involve as many of the group members as possible. This may be in the form of suggestions, advice or merely discussing the need and the possibilities of change with these individuals. This serves two purposes. First, the responsibile individual may gain some valuable insight into the impact of the change and second, the individuals being consulted will feel that they are a part of the change process and thus are more likely to accept it. This was dramatically demonstrated in the Hawthorne studies conducted in the late 1920's. Certain female workers in one of the large Western Electric plants were selected for an experiment designed to determine the relationship of working conditions to productivity. The experiment was based on changes in these conditions. Hours were changed, break periods were varied, place of work was shifted and other variables were introduced. Not only did the workers involved accept the changes, but production increased in almost every circumstance. To understand why, we must consider the manner in which the changes were made. In the first place the workers involved had been told that they would be the subject of a study and that it would involve changes. Thus, they were able to see that there was a purpose behind what was being done. In other words, the change was not change for its own sake but rather for the purpose of learning more about human behavior and its relation to assembly line type work. From the instigation of the first change and throughout the entire study, the girls felt that they were important to the experiment and were not just cogs in a large machine. Next, they were asked to express their opinions of the changes after they had been initiated. This further contributed to their feeling of status.

On the other hand, in some of the Hawthorne studies, change was resisted. In one group of fourteen men there was an attempt to increase production by offering more pay for more work. The results were not as expected. Production remained at the old rate despite the added incentive of increased pay. It was concluded that the 14 men had developed into such a cohesive group over the years that they resisted making any changes in their work patterns as none wanted to be accused by the others of being a "rate buster." Above all they had a suspicion that the real aim of management was to speed up the work rather than to improve the condition of the workers. Although the purpose of the experiment was to increase production, it would also benefit the individuals without placing any undue hardship on them. In spite of this attempt to increase production, it failed. In all probability the purpose of the study had not been properly communicated to the men involved. Thus, although the experiment could not be considered a success from the point of view of better production, it was a tremendous success from the point of view of observing human motivation. In this case, the men were more interested in being a part of the group than they were in receiving more pay.

There is another aspect of change which must be given an important place in this discussion. Not all change means abrupt or major modifications in the group process. Recently the Chief Justice of the United States Supreme Court made a speech to the members of the American Bar Association. His major point was that as population has increased and as technology has improved, the number and complexity of court cases has also increased to almost unmanageable proportions. He pointed out that the Federal and State Courts were far behind the times and had not kept pace with the changes taking place in contemporary society. He said that while we live in the age of the supermarket, the courts are still operating in the manner of the old country general store. He advocated changes in our judicial structure and procedures. His most important point insofar as the entire subject of change is concerned is that change need not be upsetting <u>as long as the continuity of the operation is maintained</u>. This is a vital consideration in planning for change. It may be compared to the repair of a portion of interstate highway. The increased flow of traffic requires a widening or some other modification of the roadway. While work is underway, traffic is temporarily rerouted around the area. Although change is taking place and although there may be some minor inconveniences for a period of time, the motorist who is affected by the change realizes that in the long run the results will be beneficial to him. While this may be easy to recognize in a physical problem of this type, it is not always easy to bring the same acceptance or understanding to problems of human behavior which may not be so apparent.

A few years ago, a large school system decided to automate many of the administrative functions within the various schools. The initial phase was to introduce a system of recording attendance and grades by use of data processing cards rather than by the old manual method. Planning for the change was complete and orderly. The teachers and administrators involved were given the necessary instruction in the use of the cards and were told why the changes were necessary. Resistance to the change was obvious on the part of many staff members, but not all of them. It was interesting to note that opposition to the new procedures did not just come from the older teachers. In fact, some of them welcomed any change that would relieve them of the drudgery of administrative tasks. Some of the younger teachers were opposed to the change while others were in favor of it. It was significant that those individuals who had had previous exposure to automation were in favor of the new procedures. In any event, the planning continued and eventually the change was made with almost predictable results. Those who had opposed the new methods had many complaints and misgivings and were very vocal in their displeasure. However, as time went by and the advantages became apparent, opposition subsided. Within a short time there was 100% agreement that the automation of school record keeping was one of the most helpful changes ever introduced into the system. New teachers coming into the system who had nothing on which to base a comparison accepted the procedures being used as the way administration should be handled.

From the foregoing we can arrive at certain conclusions. Accepting the fact that change is inevitable, we must make sure that it is implemented in an effective manner. Change should not be for the sake of change only. Changes must be dictated by a need. Next, possible changes must be evaluated to determine the most likely course of action. Certainly the next step, and a vital one, is the involvement of the people concerned. If possible, they should be consulted, but above all they should be given an honest explanation of the need for the change, the time and manner in which it is to be made and the expected results. It should be emphasized that even with this complete preparation, there might be resistance and displeasure. Much will depend on the conditions which have prevailed in the group up to this time. If the climate has been one of cooperation, mutual trust and understanding, it is much more likely that the change will be successful.

Perhaps, there is no better way to summarize this important aspect of human relations than to paraphrase the words of the great Scotch poet Robert Burns. He observed that the best laid plans of mice and men often go astray and obviously he was correct. However in the area of change, if plans are not "well laid," they will almost certainly go astray.

CHAPTER EIGHT

DECISION MAKING

All of us face decisions everyday. Many of these are so routine and inconsequential that they require little thought and are of importance only to ourselves. For example, the choice of the clothing we will wear to work of school, the selection of our lunch from the menu, the television program we will watch and similar decisions generally have little importance in the overall scheme of our lives. On the other hand we face decisions which are of tremendous importance to our present and our future. Choice of a mate, selection of our vocation, the decision as to whether to volunteer for the armed forces or wait to be drafted, the decision as to whether to pursue one course of study or another are just a few of the decisions we face that may alter the course of our lives.

At the same time there are other people making decisions which will likewise affect our lives. Various legislative bodies, the superintendent, the foreman, the commanding officer and others are in this category. In some cases the decisions are being made with little or no awareness on our part. This is true with respect to the many laws which are passed each year and which may effect us directly or indirectly. On the other hand as we move to the more personal level, we are aware that in our job or school situation people who are relatively close to us are likewise influencing our lives by the decisions they make.

Decision making is closely related to the area of change. In fact it can be said that every decision is either the result of a change in the situation or is made in order to effect change. Because of the importance of decision making in terms of its effect on human behavior, it is vital that these who are responsible for decisions understand some of the principles involved.

In the first place, decisions generally should not be made by only one person. If possible, the responsible individual should consult with those who will be affected. It is realized that this is not always possible to the degree desired. For example, the president of a large university could not consult on an individual basis with twenty to thirty thousand students. However, in the democratic tradition he could meet with representatives of groups and gain the benefit of their suggestions and observations. It would also be essential that he consider the members of his staff. This is a factor that is too often overlooked by those in authority. Even in the military, which many consider to be autocratic rather than democratic, the wise commander uses every member of his staff and as many members of his command as possible to gain information before making the final decision. Here the decision maker should realize that it is to his advantage and to the groups that he make the right decision. Thus, he should bring into use as many brains as possible. The status or rank of the individual being consulted should not be a factor. In many cases some apparently unlikely person might contribute a great idea which could be the key to the entire situation. It should, of course, be obvious that time may preclude consultation with many others. In fact, there are times when one individual may have to make the decision entirely on his own. This does not happen too often. In the hours before the Normandy invasion, General Eisenhower faced one of the most important decisions which ever confronted a military commander. Although the final decision was his responsibility alone, he took what time was available to meet with his top advisors. After weighing their counsel, he made his decision. In 1962, President Kennedy faced a crises of major proportions as Russian ships with atomic missiles rapidly approached the island of Cuba. The decision had to be made by the President. In spite of the importance of time, President Kennedy spent hours with his closest advisors and made his decision based on the best advice and the best information he could obtain. Fortunately most of us never have to face decisions which confront the President of the United States or a top military commander. However, at a lower level we do face the need for timely and workable decision making. It is important that we never loose sight of the fact that around us is a source of brain power waiting to be used. By using it we not only insure a better decision but if the individuals concerned realize that they had a part in the decision making process, they are more likely to accept it and make it work.

The leader should remember that if a situation demands a decision, one should be forthcoming as soon as practicable. Subordinates, be they students, teachers, military personnel, sons and daughters or janitors, like the feeling of security. This comes about through confidence that the leader will make a timely decision. At an early age children resent the characteristic of indecision which is present in some parents. In most cases, the child would rather be told "no" than to be left in suspense as to what the decision will be. It is extremely frustrating to work for an individual who cannot make up his mind. It is amazing to contemplate the large number of people who reach positions of policy making who continue to be indifferent to the need for timely decisions. Often they give the impression that they avoid making decisions in the hope that the problems will just go away. In some cases this actually happens, however, other problems inevitably arise and all of them will not automatically disappear.

Another factor which must be considered in decision making is that although we should aim for perfection, there will be times when the decision we make is less than perfect. In some cases, we must settle for what is workable and acceptable even though it is not ideal. Almost any decision should be subject to modification.

Thus, if we find that our decision was not the best, we should be ready to go through the same process again and make new decisions to remedy the weaknesses of the first. It must be considered that in most situations involving people, the number and types of decisions possible is almost limitless. It might be compared to a professor preparing an examination. He would like every question to be a model of clarity and purpose. He knows, however, that this will not be the case. This does not stop him from his preparation. He does the best he can and in subsequent efforts he tries to improve the product.

One pitfall in the decision making process which can negate even the best of decisions is the failure on the part of the leader or supervisor to make sure that the decision is implemented as intended. Failure to do so is very much like the difficulties in which parents find themselves with respect to the rearing of their children. The parents, after careful consideration, have decided that the son may have the family car if he meets certain requirements which have been developed between him and his parents. Both parties are satisfied with the decision. One of the requirements is that he be home no later than a given time. The son disregards this and arrives home an hour later than was agreed. The parents overlook this giving the son the impression that the decision and the agreement was not of any importance in the first place. A high school chemistry teacher did not require the students to wear safety glasses as prescribed by state law. The principal told the teacher that the glasses must be worn. This decision was final and would be enforced. After a few days the teacher reverted to the former practice of not requiring goggles. Although the principal had made the decision and was aware that it was not being followed, he did nothing about it. Not only did this weaken his position in the eyes of the teacher, but the students were also aware of this weakness. In this school it soon became apparent that although the principal and his staff made competent decisions, they were not enforced in a uniform manner thus creating an unfavorable situation among the staff, the teachers and the students.

In any organization the decision maker should recognize the needs of the organization and those of the individuals who are part of it. If he loses sight of either of these aspects of the operation, his decisions will not be very useful. His goal should be to make decisions which will let the subordinates realize that their goals and those of the group are so closely related that they are interdependent. When the group goals and the individual needs blend together as one, the result will be a harmonious operation.

The decision maker should always be willing to accept the full responsibility for the results of his decision. Even though he used his staff and others in the process, he is ultimately responsible for the success or failure of the activity. If the decision was not a good one, it is up to him to take the full responsibility without trying to blame others who helped make the decision. In other words "buck passing" is not an acceptable practice. President Harry S. Truman fully realized this. In all his public pronouncements he let it be known that he was aware of his responsibilities and would not evade them or make excuses if they were not fully implemented. To emphasize this point, he had a small sign on his desk which said, "The Buck Stops Here." By this, he meant that although others might engage in this practice, he was the one person in the United States who had no one to whom he could shift responsibility. An evaluation of Mr. Trumen's leadership qualities make it obvious that even if it had been possible for him to pass the buck, he would not have taken such an action.

The final point with respect to decision making involves the much discussed matter of communication. Frequently the complaint is heard from group members that they do not know what is going on or that they never "get the word." Too often once a decision is made the decision maker fails to insure that it is disseminated to the people concerned. Time and time again much study and planning is wasted because the eventual decision is never relayed to the proper individuals or is sent too late to be of any use. Even in this day of almost instant communication we continue to see instances of this weakness.

There is some evidence that in recent years there has been more emphasis on the importance of decision making. Many colleges and universities offer courses of study in such subjects as Business Administration, Business Management, Education Administration and other subjects in which the decision making process has a prominent place in the curriculum. In general, it can be said that we have made progress in the field, but there is much room for improvement.

CHAPTER NINE

LEADERSHIP

Because man lives and works in groups and because groups have goals or objectives, leadership becomes a necessary factor in our existence. Down through the ages we have seen the rise and fall of leaders of every description. Some have been leaders in the field of government or politics; others have been in military organizations; some have been in the church, business, sports, and in every other facet of man's acitivities. The need for effective leadership is obvious. We only have to think of the early days of this nation when so much depended upon the strength and ability of men such as Washington, Franklin, Jefferson, Monroe and others. In the great struggle between the North and South, Lincoln provided the leadership that was necessary for the preservation of the Union. Indeed when he was removed from the scene by the assassin's bullet the nation floundered and was plunged into chaos for lack of a capable replacement. All leadership, however, is not of such magnitude. In our daily routines we are exposed to leadership at all levels. Many of us hold positions of leadership in the various organizations of which we are a part. Further, and this is of great importance, in a discussion of leadership, we seem to be able to recognize the individual whom we consider a "good" leader. Likewise we can identify the individual who is not effective in his position of leadership.

There are two major considerations in dealing with the subject of leadership. First, what do we mean by a "good" leader and second, how can we develop ourselves and others to be the kind of leader we consider "good?"

Consider the question, was Adolph Hitler a good leader? During World War I, this obscure man of Austrian birth was a corporal in the German Army. After the war he remained in obscurity while he developed certain theories about power and the destiny of the German nation. In the early 1920's he was able to gather about him a handful of Germans who were attracted to him and to his ideas. By the early 1930's his followers numbered in the thousands and by 1933 he had become the master of Germany. Now through the skillful use of propaganda, pagentry, oratory, music and the appeal to national pride, he was able to turn the German people into a mightly war machine with the objective of conquering the world. His ability to influence people was so great that he gained the support of every segment of the population. Of course, we know how his plan of conquest failed. In the end with the entire nation in ruins around him and most of his military forces dead, captured or ineffective, he took his own life within a bomb shelter in Berlin. Now again we ask the question, was he a good leader? Immediately we see that the word good has two meanings. It can mean good morally or good in the sense of effective. To judge the morality of a leader is often dangerous but in the case of Hitler we are safe in saying that any man who was able to have about 6,000,000 Jews exterminated would hardly be described as moral. Then we might ask was he effective. Any one who lived through those years prior to World War II or anyone who has viewed the record of the Nazi movement on film has to be impressed with the magnitism which Hitler exuded as he lead a nation which had been defeated in 1918 to a position of world strength by 1939. But, as we look at the entire record, we again see the total and complete failure he experienced and again we are left with the question, was he a good leader?

Throughout the years the government, the military, industry and other groups have been in constant search for leaders. Millions of dollars are spent each year in various types of schools which are supposed to teach leadership. Countless man hours have been spent in research in an effort to develop a more certain way to produce the leaders who are needed so desperately. Large corporations regard leadership at the top and all the way down to the smallest group as essential to the effective operation of the organization.

The problem of defining leadership and developing leaders may be expressed rather simply. Although we can list the attributes of a good leader and although we can name individuals who are acknowledged to be good leaders, we still do not have the formula for producing this type of person. In fact, we continually hear the question, "are leaders born or are they made?" and the argument continues with some advocates of each position and some who say that both apply.

The word charisma has become a popular one in recent years as a term which applies to a person who has the qualities of leadership. Most people agree with John F. Kennedy, Dwight D. Eisenhower, Martin Luther King, Billy Graham and a few others of our time have had this attribute. At the same time many would say that Lyndon Johnson, Richard Nixon and the Reverand James Abernathy do not have this trait. When we try to arrive at a definition of what charisma is, we can find no conclusive answer. Most people would say that it is something about the person which attracts and hold followers. This, of course, is what a leader should do, but how and why does this charisma come about? It might also be asked whether charisma is an essential ingredient in leadership. Is it not possible for Mr. Nixon to be an effective president and be the leader of his nation and his party without this intangible quality?

Because the military has had so much experience with leadership and leadership development, it might be well to look at some of the qualities which are considered to be essential in the effecti military commander. Military leadership has been defined as "the art of influencing and directing others to an assigned goal in such a manner as to command their obediance, confidence, respect, and loyal cooperation."[8] In this we can see that military leadership is not any different from that in civilian life as certainly the civilian leader should have the same objectives. Indeed a recent definition of leadership by social scientists who have done much research on the subject is "the performance of functions which help a group to achieve its objectives."[9] It has been said that military leaders should have certain qualities. They are self confidence, experience, decisiveness, initiative, resourcefulness, thoughtfulness, impartiality, integrity, dependability and sincerity. Others are also considered desirable but this is enough to point out that the standards as set by the military are indeed comprehensive and for many individuals difficult to attain. On the other hand, it follows that the qualities enumerated are certainly desirable in all individuals. Further could not a person possess all of these traits and still not be a good leader?

In the study of leadership there is yet another aspect which makes any scientific analysis most difficult. This can best be illustrated by taking a look at two of the great leaders of World War II. One of these commanded the Third United States Army in Europe. His name was Patton. The other commanded the First United States Army, also in Europe, his name was Hodges. It is doubtful that many readers will recognize the latter name, but all know the name of Patton. In fact even during World War II the name Hodges was little known while that of his more famous contemporary was constantly before the people of the world. Patton was flamboyant, and dramatic in everything he did. The very uniforms he wore seemed to add to his stature as a combat leader. He gloried in his position and was always available to the members of the press who in turn found that the public was always ready to read about his exploits. Call it charisma, call it color, call it what you will, Patton will go down in history as one of our great military leaders. Hodges had a very similar military background to Patton's. Both attended West Point* and other army service schools. Both had made their way through the various grades in the peace time army when promotions were few and far between. Both had been recognized by their superiors as leaders of great potential and both became four star generals in command of field armies in the biggest war in the history of man. Hodges was almost shy. He seldom sought publicity and the press seldom sought him. He dressed in the manner of an average soldier, no special uniforms or fancy trappings for him. He seldom raised his voice and his vocabulary lacked the impact of Patton's. We would be quite surprised if there were ever a movie called "Hodges" while Patton has already been immortalized in color by Hollywood. In other words, on the surface we find two men as different in their personalities

*Hodges did not graduate.

and characteristics as we could hope to find, yet each was a great success as a military leader. As a matter of fact it could be said that Courtney Hodges was a much better leader as he carried out his mission without causing his superiors the anxious moments and problems provided by Patton. Further, although Patton was able to instill in his men the importance of the group objectives, he did so in such a way that he was feared more than he was respected. Hodges on the other hand was able to instill the same motivation in his troops without using the methods implied in the nickname by which Patton was known, "old blood and guts."

Hundreds of examples could be given from both military and civilian life to show that leaders do not fit into any particular mold which can be analyzed, described and then used as a model. In fact, recent studies have reaffirmed what has been known for many years that "there is no single leadership type of personality."[10] That is why we find successful leaders from every segment of our society. In our leaders we see represented every level of education socio-economic background, ethnic group, political philosophy, intelligence, and moral character.

With the foregoing in mind, let us take a look at the problem of training leaders. If there is no set type of leadership personality, is it not then possible to take almost anyone and train him to be a leader? There are many who would answer this in the affirmative. Many people must believe that such training is possible otherwise government and industry would not be spending millions of dollars each year on leadership training programs.

Again we look at the military to observe the results of this type of training. For well over one hundred years the Army and the Navy have maintained service academies which have achieved world wide renown. West Point and Annapolis have become almost synonymous with the production of outstanding leaders. More recently the Air Force has established and developed its own program at the Air Force Academy in Colorado. To enter one of these three schools, the individual must meet most stringent requirements. Upon enrolling he begins four years of continuous and intensive training in many area but above all the subject of leadership has always been most important. Given such a set of circumstances, it would be thought that by the time the individual had survived the physical and academic rigors of the four year program and was graduated as an officer in the armed forces, he would have become an outstanding leader or at least have the necessary training to become one. While it is true that the number of leaders produced by these service academies has been large, it is also true that many never achieved the potential expected of them and others were actually ineffective when put to the test of actual military leadership. On the other hand, many individuals in the Army, Navy and Air Force have become outstanding leaders not only without the benefit of the academy training, but with very little formal training at all.

Finally, many studies of leadership contain lists of qualities, procedures, or principles which are considered essential to being a good leader. As has been previously indicated not only are these traits extremely idealistic, but it would be difficult to achieve unanimous agreement on the list or on the meaning of each term. It is possible, however, to establish certain guidelines which seem to be part of effective leadership.

1. The goals of the group must always be the primary consideration of an effective leader.

2. Although the group objectives are paramount, individual group members have needs which must be met if at all possible. Group members may wish to express themselves concerning group procedures. They might want to be considered in the decision making process. Above all they will want to be kept informed as to the activities of the group and the progress being made.

3. Leaders must constantly evaluate group functions and activities. If changes are indicated, they must be able to initiate them in the most effective manner possible.

4. The appointed or elected leader must never forget that although he may and should delegate authority, the responsibility for the group and its progress rests with him. He must take the responsibility for the outcome of the operation without shifting the blame to someone else.

CHAPTER TEN

UNDERSTANDING RACIAL DISCRIMINATION

Of all the words used to describe man, one of the most misunderstood is the term "race." Today more than ever before, we in the United States have become race conscious largely due to the many disturbing events which have taken place in the past ten to fifteen years involving black-white relationships. These events have been primarily of two types. The first would include the legal measures which have been taken in the area of civil rights. These include not only the many laws which have been enacted by national and state legislatures, but also the numerous decisions which have been made by federal and state courts. It is not our purpose to discuss these legal measures in detail or to judge their merits. The fact remains that regardless of our opinions, they have become part of the law of the land and as has been demonstrated are subject to enforcement by government agencies. It is enough to say that most of these measures were enacted in order to insure that members of all minority groups would enjoy the rights and privileges of any other citizen.

The second type of event which has emerged from the status of blacks and whites in the United States is that which can be classified as illegal. This would include the large scale riots in Watts, Detroit, Newark, Cleveland and elsewhere in which lives were lost and property destroyed. It would also include the more localized actions on the part of certain individuals such as the murder of Martin Luther King, Medger Evers and the three "freedom marchers" in Mississippi. While these acts are readily apparent and received wide publicity, it is obvious that they are just a small part of the total picture of racial trouble in our nation today. There is the continuing controversy on court ordered school integration and the busing which is required. There is the open or thinly disguised animosity of the whites for the blacks and the blacks for the whites. Out of this, have come derogatory words which are used as labels to identify members of each group. Some of these words have been a part of the American language for many years. "Nigger" or "coon" are just two of these the history of which extends far back into the past. "Whitey" or "Honkie" are similar terms used by blacks to show contempt for whites. On every hand we see a lack of trust on the part of one group for the other.

Although the problems today are largely those which exist between the blacks and the whites, the history of our country shows that at various times there were other minority groups which were the targets of hatred, prejudice and discrimination on the part of individuals who considered themselves "100% Americans." Thus, in the latter half of the nineteenth century there was a fear on the part of so called "native" Americans that the influx of large numbers of foreigners constituted a threat to their economic security.

Not only was there a systematic effort to exclude foreigners, but the various minority groups already in the United States were the target of animosity from the members of the majority. It is also significant to note that members of minorities were prejudiced against other minorities. This is an interesting point when it is considered that practically all of the members of these minorities could be classified as Caucasoids (white) and were members of religious denominatinos which, if not Christian, were at least supposed to believe in the same God. Even today in some parts of the country there remains prejudice against various groups and individuals because of their place of origin or religious beliefs.

Although most of our problems seem to be concerned with the relationship of blacks and whites, it must be remembered that prejudice is not limited to this situation. For example, at the present time in certain parts of Florida and in New York City where there has been an influx of Cubans and Puerto Ricans we see discrimination at work. In the southwest and in certain location on the west coast, many members of the majority group look down upon Mexicans or Mexican-Americans. Of course, the most glaring example of all might be the manner in which the only true native American, the Indian, has been, and is being treated, by many fellow Americans.

We should make it clear that such problems are not unique to the United States. The war in South East Asia has demonstrated that people of the same race who are very similar in physical characteristics, cultural background and religion can be bitter toward each other because of their national origin. Thus, we see the extreme hatred between the Cambodians and the Vietnamese or the Koreans and the Japanese. History records other such hatreds which have existed for generations. In a country as small as Belgium there are intense feelings between the Walloons and the Flemish. Both are Caucasoids, both are Belgian nationals, both call themselves Christians but they regard each other as inferior and have little friendly contact. Ireland provides another example where in the nation is divided and has suffered greatly because of religious differences which go back beyond the memory of any living person.

In the United States today and in much of the rest of the world one of the primary sources of prejudice is the conflict between races. To understand the meaning of this term it will be necessary to use material from the fields of anthropology, biology, sociology and psychology all of which are concerned with various aspects of human life. The term race as used with reference to man is a scientific attempt to place him in various groups according to physical characteristics. Note the word physical as this is one of the keys to the understanding of what will be discussed. Biologists classify all living things in an attempt to show kinship. Thus, man belongs to the order known as primates which also include such animals as monkeys, apes and marmosets. Within the family* divisions are made according to genus. Man is considered to be genus Homo which is the Latin word meaning man. Within genra (plura for genus) are species. Man belongs to the species Homo Sapiens which means "man the wise." Now for another important concept in this discussion of race. All men are included in the same family, genus and species regardless of skin color, type of hair, shape of the skull, eyes or nose.

One of the many problems encountered in a study of race is that of number. How many races of mankind are there? Experts cannot agree. To show how diverse opinion is, estimates vary from the belief that there is really only one race to as many as 37 or 38. From the human relations point of view we will think in terms of three major races. These are referred to as the Caucasoid (like the Caucasian), the Mongoloid (like the Mongolian), and the Negroid (like the Negro). These three categories are often commonly (but not correctly) referred to as the white, the yellow and the black races. Over the years extensive studies have been made in an effort to scientifically isolate the physical characteristics of each race so that ready and positive identification could be made. Some of the features studied have been skin color, stature, head form, hair color, hair texture, hair form (straight, wavy, kinky), eye color and the shape of the nose.

Skin color is perhaps the most obvious means by which the layman identifies race even though it is most unrealiable. The skin of natives of India vary from light to dark. Many of them are as dark as members of the Negroid race. However, the Indian is classified as a Caucasoid. On the other hand, there are many individuals in the world today who are classified as Negroids who have skin which is lighter than many Caucasoids. Further, and this is significant, although Caucasoids think of themselves as "white" they are in fact anything from pale pink to brown. The only true whites on earth are people who lack any skin pigmentation at all. These individuals are called albinos and this condition occurs among the darkest people of Africa as it does among Caucasoids in the United States.

Although skin color is extremely unreliable as an indicator of race, it is used by many individuals because it is so obvious. Biologists regard skin color as a result of natural selection and a factor in survival. Dark skinned people live in areas which are generally tropical and thus extremely warm. They are exposed to the rays of the sun much more than are the individuals who live in the temperate zones. Black skin becomes an asset to the individual in the hot regions of the world. It is ironic to observe how many

*Hominidae is man's family classification.

"whites" spend much of their time each summer trying to darken their skin by exposure to the sun and/or through the use of chemical preparations. It is also interesting to note that members of the Negroid race have more sweat glands than do members of the other two races. Here again nature has helped insure survival by furnishing people who live in the tropics with additional cooling devices. The broad nostrils of dark skinned people are also considered an additional survival feature in that this type of nose is better adapted to the intake of warm damp air than is the narrower nose of the Caucasoid.

There are many individuals today who equate a person's dark skin to a closer relationship with other animals, especially the apes and monkeys. Actually from a biological point of view, it is the Caucasoid who most resembles the apes, monkeys and other anthrapoids. A few points are worthy of mention with regard to this often overlooked fact. Members of the so-called white race are hairer than either the Negroids or the Mongoloids. The latter two races have little body hair. A further note of interest in the matter of hair has to do with the type which man possesses as compared with other animals. It can be easily demonstrated that the lank hair of the Caucasoid is much more like that of the anthrapoids than is the kinky hair of the Negroid. Lips of members of the white race are thin and narrow as are those of apes, monkies and gorillas.

Such comparisons actually should have no bearing on the judging of other human beings. They are introduced here to emphasize that commonly held ideas are often not supported by the available evidence. Do the similarities between the Caucasoids and certain other animals mean that the white man is closer to these animals than is the black? Of course not. However, many people with racial prejudice maintain that the black man most resembles the apes and thus is an inferior being.

There are several theories as to why differences occurred which resulted in the various racial groupings. One is that as man wandered over the face of the earth and settled in new regions, he adjusted over a long period of time to his physical environment through physical changes. Another explanation might be found in the occurrence of mutations which were than perpetuated. A mutation is a condition in which a particular gene undergoes a permanent change which is expressed in a new trait or characteristic. For example, if all men at one time had the same color skin, mutations could have taken place which resulted in offspring of a different color. This new color was then genetically transmitted to subsequent generations. Still another theory is that the three races of man originated in widely separated parts of the world possibly at about the same time. Although natural scientists may debate various theories and findings concerning physical differences, from the viewpoint of human relations, the important fact is that such differences do exist and do affect our opinions, our judgments and our attitudes toward those who differ from our preconceived ideas of what is "best."

In his book <u>Man's Most Dangerous Myth</u>: <u>The Fallacy of Race</u>, Ashley Montagu makes a strong plea for better understanding of what race really means. One of his major points is that as we study the various types of humans in the world we are confronted by the fact that from an anatomical point of view there are many more similarities than there are differences.[11] Further the differences can be described as superficial. Man makes no judgment about the quality of horses based on the color of the horse's hair covering. He is interested in a horse which will either be a good racer, jumper or work animal regardless of his color. The same can be said about man's judgment of dogs. It makes little difference if the pointer or setter has a red coat, a white coat or one which is black and white. However, in the far more important realm of human evaluation man is ready to make his judgment based on skin color alone. As has been mentioned, the use of physical characteristics to determine race is questionable and yet not only is it used by many, but such criteria can be found in what might be considered an authoritative work. The following quotation illustrates this point. "All the modern varieties of mankind are included in the single species, Homo Sapiens. The major racial characteristics today are, of course easily distinguishable by superficial differences such as those of skin pigmentation, hair texture, nose shape, etc., but it is not possible so readily to distinguish them on internal anatomical characteristics. Contrary to popular supposition even the racial differences in the skull are often so poorly defined as to make a racial diagnosis on cranial evidence alone very uncertain."[12] The point of this quotation is well taken in one respect in that it emphasizes the likeness of races insofar as internal physical characteristics are concerned. However, it is misleading in that it states that it is easy to identify race by the superficial traits mentioned.

Much is often made of the fact that the average cranial capacity of the black man is some fifty cubic centimeters less than the average for whites. This has been used by some as proof that blacks do not have as much intelligence as whites. Such arguments become meaningless when we compare the modern white man with the very primitive Neanderthal men who lived more than fifty thousand years ago. Skulls of those remote beings have indicated that they had an average cranial capacity of 1550 cc as compared with the average for modern Caucasoids of 1400 cc. Certainly we cannot conclude from this that the Neanderthal man was superior in intelligence to modern man. The fact is that size of cranium has not been related to intelligence. Further, we are not sure as to how much intelligence is due to heredity and how much to environment. Suffice to say that high and low and all in between intelligence quotients (IQ's) have been found in all races.

Montagu concludes that prejudice is the sign of an incompletely developed personality. The person who is racially prejudiced (or prejudiced in other ways) has not learned the fundamental facts concerning the nature of human beings including himself.[13]

Although it is possible to recognize some physical differences among the races, it must again be emphasized that these are superficial. Skin color has already been discussed. What then are some of the other differences? Mongoloids have a small fold of skin over the inner corner of the eye formed by an extension of the upper lid. This is called the epicanthic fold and gives orientals the distinctive appearance often referred to as "slant-eyed" by non-orientals. Often this term is used to imply an inferiority in appearance, ability, behavior, character or some other trait. Many American military men who have served in the Far East were rather shocked to learn that the orientals referred to them as "round-eyes" and that this was also a term which was not complimentary. We might well ask what difference does a small fold of skin makes when we consider the entire person?

Another physical difference which has been found is that among Negroes certain bones of the foot are formed somewhat differently than are those of non-Negroes. This is a fairly recent discovery. Again we might ask what difference does this make and who is to say which foot is the best?

Taking a look at the physical ways in which the races are alike, we find that in those aspects which are important to life itself, there is absolutely no difference among the races. Blood is a good example. We hear the term "Negro blood," "Chinese blood," "White blood," "Indian blood" and so on. There is no such division of blood from the scientific point of view. It is all human blood and there is no way that the blood of a Negroid, a Mongoloid or a Caucasoid can be distinguished one from the other. Blood, as long as it is of the same chemical blood group, can be transfused with that of another human being regardless of the race of the donor. In the United States today when blood is used in transfusions, it is quite possible that the person who gave the blood was of a different race than the one receiving it. It must be emphasized that traits are transmitted through <u>genes</u> not blood.

During World War II, blood was of great concern to Hitler and he issued orders to insure that members of what he termed "the Master Race" would under no circumstances receive blood from a Jewish donor. This is a significant commentary on the myth of race when it is considered that many of the world's greatest scientists in all fields, including medicine, have been natives of Germany or of German descent. In fact the Germans have often been stereotyped as scientifically gifted people. However, because of Hitler's power, these supposedly scientific Germans accepted the concept of a master race while Jews and their blood were placed in an inferior category. Official German policy prohibited the marriage of Jews and non-Jews so that the purity of "the German race" would be preserved.

Although we may consider these edicts of Nazi dictatorship as scientifically unsound, the laws in many of our own states have been just as lacking in sceintific accuracy. As many as nineteen states have had laws forbidding marriages on the grounds of race.[14] It has only been in recent years that such laws have been declared unconstitutional in that they violated a fundamental right of free men, namely the selection of a mate. It is interesting to note that while in all of the nineteen states marriages between whites and blacks were prohibited, some permitted unions between whites and Mongoloids. Some states legislated against marriages between whites and American Indians while others held these to be legal. It is significant that the laws pertaining to marriage were very vague in most cases with respect to race determination. Some had such descriptions as "A person of color" (Louisiana);" any mulatto, half bread, Indian, Negro or mestizo" (South Carolina). Others used as a criteria the amount of "Negro" blood which a person possessed. In most cases it was legally established that a person with one-eighth or more of Negro (or in some cases Mongolian) blood was non-white. Thus a person who was seven-eighths "white" would be classified as a "black." Some states were even more inclusive with such definitions of a "white person" as "such person who has no trac whatever of any blood other than Caucasian" (Virginia). Just how this "trace" of blood was to be determined is not clear. In any event such laws remained in effect in the United States until very recently and although they may have effectively prevented mixed marriages in many areas of the country, it is obvious that they did not prevent sexual contact between the races.

In the process of human reproduction, as in the case of blood, there is no difference between the races. Because we all belong to the same species, we can have sexual intercourse with a member of any of the other races and we can produce offspring who are in turn capable of normal reproduction. This, probably more than any other factor, identifies all men as being physically the same in the most basic of all life processes. In the animal world, it is extremely rare to find sexual relations between species. In those unusual instances where this does occur, either no offspring result or if there are offspring, they are often sterile. The prime example of this is the mating of the horse and the donkey which produces the sterile mule.

Before going further, it should be stated that the writers are in no way evaluating the rightness or wrongness of the interracial mixing which has taken and is taking place. There are members of all races who do not advocate further interracial mixing. During the past thirty years the United States has fought three conflicts in which many Americans were sent to various parts of the world. As in every war soldiers far from home sought and gained the favors of the native women. Thus in the islands of South Pacific, throughout Japan and on the mainland of Asia, the white and the black American soldier has left his offspring. Not all of these relationships were temporary as we note the large number of "war brides" who returned to the United States.

A related and important factor in discussing the likeness of race is that at time of conception we are all basically alike. When the male sperm unites with the ovum of the female, the result is a single cell containing forty-six chromosomes with twenty-three being provided by each parent. This is true regardless of the racial mixture of the mating individuals. This further emphasizes the point that we are all members of the human race and as such have much more in common in the important aspects of life than we have differences.

All of the foregoing is evidence that the outward physical characteristics of race are indeed unimportant when compared to those which are esential to life itself. In spite of this there are many members of all races who disregard this evidence and persist in retaining preconceived ideas concerning the merits or demerits of being a member of a given race.

Thus far we have looked primarily at race from a physical point of view, but we cannot understand prejudice unless we examine certain historical facts which have influenced the racial situation in the United States today.

Students of human relations should realize that prejudice exists in our minds because of ignorance, fear or both. It is only through a better understanding of others that we will be able to make any progress toward the elimination of this problem-causing aspect of human behavior.

Negroes were in this country before the Mayflower landed at Plymouth Rock. In 1619 twenty blacks arrived at Jamestown, Virginia. Most U.S. history books indicate that these blacks probably were brought to the new world in a Dutch warship and that they were sold as slaves to the white colonists. Recently, however, evidence has been presented to show that these African natives were not slaves but rather indentured servants. The difference between a slave and an indentured servant is an important one. A slave was regarded as chattel or property. As such he was owned by a master, had no rights as a human being and had no control over his activities or his future. He was in bondage forever or at the discretion of his owner. An indentured servant, on the other hand, had made a legal contract in which he had received transportation to America and other consideration in exchange for a stated number of years (usually 7) in the service of his benefactor. At the end of the designated time, the individual achieved his complete freedom. Whether the first blacks in America were slaves or indentured servants is an academic question at this time. The fact remains that shortly after 1619, more and more blacks were brought from Africa to America and they were brought here as slaves.

Slavery flourished in the colonies and when independence from England was finally won in 1781, this "peculiar institution" continued to be a part of the economic and social life of the new nation. Although it was most prevalent in the south, it was legal throughout the thirteen states.

The history of slavery in the United States is long, complicated and important. Although the Declarations of Independence contained the noble phrase that "All men are created equal," we know that this equality did not refer to civil equality. Thomas Jefferson, the chief author of the Declaration, was himself a slave holder as were many of the men who are revered as the founders of our country. When in 1787 the United States Constitution was presented to the thirteen states as a proposed supreme law of the land, it contained provisions which in effect acknowledged the existence and the legality of slavery. It is significant to note that neither the word slave not slavery appears in the body of the Constitution nor in the first ten amendments. However, Article One, Section Two clearly recognizes the existence of several categories in the computation of representatives and direct taxes. The phrase reads "... free person, including those bound to service for a term of years, and excluding Indians not taxed, three-fifths of all other persons." The persons bound to service for a term of years were the indentured servants while the "other persons" were the slaves. Thus we can see that although a representative form of government was established, it was by no means a complete democracy. One of the major debates at the constitutional convention was the status of slaves. Were they people or were they property? This debate placed the slave holding states in a delemna. If the slaves were property, they could not be people. Thus they could not be counted in the population of the slave holding states. This would, of course, reduce the number of legislators these states could send to the House of Representatives. If, on the other hand, they were people, they would have to be counted for purposes of taxation which would mean that the southern states would have to contribute more to the federal government. The delemna was resolved by the "three-fifths" compromise. Only three-fifths of the "other persons" (slaves) were to be counted for the purpose of apportioning representatives and direct taxes. This clearly shows that slavery was acknowledged as a fact of life by those early Americans of power and influence.

Some members of the convention wanted the Constitution to include a provision which would end the importation of slaves. Again the slave holding states would not agree to such a proposal. After much debate another compromise was reached which further recognized the legality of slavery. Article I, Section 9 contains thi statement, "The migration or importation of such persons as any of the states now existing shall think proper to admit, shall not be prohibited by the Congress prior to the year one thousand eight hundred and eight, but a tax or duty may be imposed on such importation, not exceeding ten dollars for each person." Thus, the importation of slaves was to continue for 21 years from the date of the signing of the Constitution.

If the foregoing bit of history concerning slavery in the colonies and at the time of the Constitutional Convention seems to contradict some of the democratic principles we may have long cherished, it should be remembered that while the slaves were indeed in a most inhuman and often inhumane status in the early days of this nation, so were certain other groups. Certainly the status of Indians is revealed in the portion of the Constitution quoted above. Those few who were taxed had some legal status but the vast majority might be regarded as non-persons. They had very few rights and certainly were not participating members in this new government. Women likewise were discriminated against and it was not until many years later (1920) that they were given the right to vote.

Slavery flourished and its existence was to cause this nation to fight a tragic civil war which would lead to a chaotic reconstruction period and a dangerous racial situation which has persisted to this day. Slavery did more than enslave men's bodies. It had social and psychological effects on both whites and blacks which have seriously handicapped progress in the field of race relations. It is most difficult for the black of today to forget that his ancestors were considered less than human by white slave owners. Added to this embitterment is the fact that even after a war had been fought, the Constitution amended, laws passed and court decisons made, blacks were still denied the rights of other citizens. It is little wonder that in recent years civil rights movements have gained so many followers.

Slavery not only denied the legal existence of blacks, but it systematically perpetuated feelings of inferiority. Today there are many whites in the United States who point to the failure of negroes to maintain stable family relationships. They describe the black man as being irresponsible and unable or unwilling to take his place as the head of the household, leaving economic affairs and the rearing of children in the hands of the women. Statistics would seem to support this when it is considered that one in four black homes is headed by a female while the ratio is one in ten for whites. Under slavery, the formation of families was most difficult. The men were not permitted to assume their role as patriarch and provider. Men were most useful as workers and thus were subject to sale. Women on the otherhand were important as producers of more slaves. The major function of the male slave in the family organization was to impregnate the females. He could experience none of the events which are so important to a man's feelings of worth in the eyes of his family. It is no wonder that much of this feeling remains today. Observation might be made that this all happened over 100 years ago so what does it have to do with the present? Social changes come about slowly. Although the blacks were technically free after 1862, it is a well known fact that for most of them there was no freedom of opportunity for self advancement. Through a system of political, economic, educational and social restrictions, the black man continued to remain at a disadvantage and many remain so today. It takes time for attitudes to change. Laws can be passed and court decisions made, and while they may help the cause of equality, much more is required. Change must take place in the hearts and minds of men before those words of hope in the Declarations of Independence can have real meaning in our lives.

The effect of slavery on the whites in the south was also pronounced. It was discouraging enough to be a member of a defeated confederation but added to this was the fact that a way of life had ended. The well-to-do land and slave owners were economically ruined by the war and its aftermath. They had regarded the slaves as their property and they attached a value to that property. Now it was gone forever. As to the poor white who might never have owned a slave, he was now in a position which placed him at the bottom of the social and economic ladder. Previously he could at least look upon the slaves as being inferior to him but now they had gained legal equality. In view of this, it can be understood why the dominent white philosophy in the south could be stated in the phrase that the black man, although free, must be "kept in his place." From this developed the doctrine of "separate but equal." Under this doctrine the south became a divided region marked by signs which read "White" and "Colored." Schools, busses, trains, restaurants, recreational facilities, churches, neighborhoods and every aspect of life maintained complete segregation of the races. When the "separate but equal" doctrine was finally challenged in 1896, it was upheld by the U.S. Supreme Court. It was not until the famous case of Brown vs. The Board of Education of Topeka in 1954 that the issue was again brought before out nation's highest tribunal. This time the decision reflected the times and it was held that facilities which were separate were inherently unequal. States were ordered to integrate their schools with "all deliberate speed." Thus, almost one hundred years after the end of the Civil War, the problem of the races continued to be a major source of trouble and frustration in the United States. Unfortunately the problem is still with us and although there has been progress, much remains to be accomplished in the field of civil rights and race relations.

Many criticisms have been directed toward the negroes in the United States in an attempt to "prove" that they are inferior to whites. Critics point to the high rate of crime, drug addiction, prostitution, illegitimacy and unemployment among blacks and conclude that this situation exists because of racial traits. To do this is to disregard all the other factors which produce anti-social behavior. There are many whites who commit crimes, become addicted to drugs, produce illegitimate offspring and desert their families. On the other hand, there are many blacks who have overcome the deprivation of their circumstances and risen to places of distinction in our country and in the world. It should be obvious that it is environment rather than race which is the major determinent in the behavior of both blacks and whites. The people who live in the decaying or decayed inner cites regardless of race, or national background certainly produce most of our social problems. A person who has never lived in a deprived environment cannot imagine the depressing effect it has on its inhabitants. The wonder is that any of these deprived people make it at all and it is especially remarkable that any blacks can escape from the grip of their environment and become successful citizens.

The black man in American had many factors operating against him. The conditions surrounding slavery were certainly most depressing and legal freedom did not bring much improvement, but the greatest liability that he had was the very color of his skin. In his book Beyond Racism[15], Young emphasizes the reality of being black. Although the immigrants from Europe were at a disadvantage upon arrival in America, it was only a temporary condition. Initially they could be easily recognized by their old-world clothes, their broken speech and their odd names. In time, however, they melted into the American scene. Certainly their children and their grandchildren came to be regarded as Americans. Style of dress is easily modified, accents are lost, names might even be changed and before long the man from Poland, Ireland, Germany or Russia no longer stands out in the crowd. Negroes on the other hand, could never really blend in. Although they had been in this country from the earliest days, they were still black and thus could be readily identified and discriminated against. Of course, there have been unknown numbers of "blacks" who have been light skinned enough to "pass" for whites but this obviously was not possible for most negroes. So we see that the accident of birth which produced a black skin made it almost impossible for the negro to be assimilated into the life of the United States whereas the white person from any other part of the world would eventually be completely integrated.

It is interesting to note that although there have been various actions of discrimination against orientals in this country, for some reason, again probably the background of slavery, they have generally been more accepted in our society than has the black man.

Until more people in the world recognize that what we do and how we act is not due to racial inheritance but rather to intelligence, education, family background, religious training and the entire environment, we will continue to have the problems which have persisted for so long in the United States and in other countries.

Students of human relations should realize that prejudice exists in our minds because of ignorance, fear or both. It is only through a better understanding of others that we will be able to make any progress toward the elimination of this problem causing aspect of human behavior.

CHAPTER ELEVEN

EFFECTIVE HUMAN RELATIONS: GUIDELINES

One of the dangers in trying to list or summarize concepts in human relations is that too often the writer falls into the dangerous practice of setting forth certain general ideas as if they are the final word in people to people relationships. To this danger is added the tendency on the part of the reader to accept such a listing as an authoritative list which merely has to be understood and applied. This is not the case. If a course or a text in human relations teaches anything, it is that there is no easy or ready made solution to the problems we face as human beings. If such solutions were available, we would have eliminated the problems a long time ago.

Thus, the list that follows is not to be accepted as all inclusive or all effective. It should be regarded as a tool for the better understanding of how we might avoid problems or how, once they have developed, they might be solved.

1. All people are different in two basic aspects. One, they do not perceive a situation in the same way and two, they have all come from different environments.

2. People usually act in a manner which makes sense to them even if their actions are based on emotions rather than on reason.

3. We communicate with each other not by words along. Our facial expression, tone of voice and general attitude influence the way in which we communicate.

4. Communication involves listening as well as talking. People have a tendency to be selective in their listening. They hear what they want to hear.

5. Human behavior is often unpredictable, however, predictability may be improved by an increased understanding of this behavior.

6. In order to understand another person's actions or motives, we must try to look at the situation from his point of view. Most of us find this extremely difficult.

7. Although man is a gregarious animal, he has strong feelings of individuality. Further he usually considers the actions and beliefs of his group to be correct when compared to groups which he regards as "foreign."

8. History shows that people can change their attitudes and outlooks. However, the process may be long and difficult and in many cases individuals will not make such changes.

9. Before a person can change, he must reach a point where he feels uncomfortable in his beliefs.

10. The more we discuss a problem, the more we tend to become concerned with a part of it thus losing sight of the total situation.

11. Although all people may not desire recognition in the usual sense of the word, it can be said that most humans would like to be treated with respect and dignity.

12. Observers may consider a person's problem in the abstract or even regard it as "no problem," however, to the individual concerned, it is specific and real.

13. Unless man finds a better way to resolve his individual differences, the world will continue to face the same perplexing human problems that have existed and are in existence today.

FOOTNOTES

CHAPTER ONE - Problem Solving

1. Advertisement, *Memphis*, July, 1970, p. 62.
2. Stuart Chase, *The Proper Study of Mankind* (New York: Harper and Row, Inc., 1956), p. 3.
3. Roger J. Williams, *You are Extraordinary* (New York: Random House, 1967), p. 214.
4. "Children Testing Proposed," *The Daily Press* (Newport News, Va.), April 12, 1970, p. 1.

CHAPTER THREE - Perception, The Great Variable

5. "Jerry West Truly Laker's Mr. Clutch," *The Daily Press* (Newport News, Va.), March 14, 1970, p. 2].
6. "Bill Dana Ends Jose Jiminez Role," *The Daily Press* (Newport News, Va.), July 6, 1970, p. 11.
7. "Harris Survey," *The Daily Press* (Newport News, Va.), July 6, 1970, p. 12.

CHAPTER NINE - Leadership

8. Senior ROTC Manual (Washington, D.C.: Department of the Army GPO, 1950), p. 1.
9. Malcolm S. Knowles, *The Leader Looks at Self Development*, Leadership Series (Washington, D.C.: Leadership Resources, Inc.. 1961), p. 1.
10. Knowles, p. 1.

CHAPTER TEN - Understanding Racial Discrimination

11. Asley Montagu, *Man's Most Dangerous Myth: The Fallacy of Race* (New York: World Publishing Co., 1964), p. 85.
12. "Man," *Encyclopedia Americana*, 1969.

13. Montagu, p. 175.
14. Montagu, p. 421
15. Whitney M. Young, Jr., <u>Beyond</u> <u>Racism</u> (New York: McGraw Hill, 1969.

GLOSSARY

It should be noted that these definitions provide a "working" tool only. In some instances there is not complete agreement concerning the definition.

ANTHROPOLOGY - The study of man. This is a most comprehensive discipline which deals with man in both his physical and sociocultural aspects.

BEHAVIORAL SCIENCES - A term which has come into use since about 1950 to describe the study of human behavior by scientific methods. The behavioral sciences are usually considered to include Sociology, Anthropology and Psychology.

CULTURE - All the behavior exhibited by a society. Includes ideas, values, customs, dress, language, art, etc. Sometimes called the cement which binds a society together.

ECONOMICS - The study of the allocation of scarce resources among unlimited and competing uses. Deals with the ways in which men and societies seek to satisfy their material needs and desires since the means at their disposal do not permit them to do so completely.

GROUP - Two or more individuals held together by common social ties.

NEUROSIS - (Psychoneurosis) Mental or nervous disorders which do not seem to have any organic cause. Usually not as serious as psychosis.

PERSONALITY - The end result of the ways in which a person reacts. The product of his motivations, emotions, style of thinking and attitudes. It is probably the product of both inborn characteristics and environment.

POLITICAL SCIENCE - The study of governmental institutions.

PSYCHIATRIST - A medical doctor who specializes in mental and emotional illnesses.

PSYCHIATRY - A field of medicine concerned with the treatment and prevention of mental diseases or disorders. Sometimes referred to as a mixture of biology, psychology, and sociology.

PSYCHOLOGIST - A specialist in psychology. Does not have to be a medical doctor, however, some psychologists are qualified to act as therapists.

PSYCHOLOGY - The study of the behavior of living organisms. (More particularly the study of the behavior of man). There are several subdivisions some of which are:
- APPLIED PSYCHOLOGY - The professional practice of personnel management, consumer behavior, counseling, etc.
- CLINICAL PSYCHOLOGY - Sometimes considered a part of the applied psychology. Clinical psychology is concerned with the diagnosis and treatment of behavior problems. In some cases clinical psychologists are qualified to treat patients in psychotherapy sessions.
- CHILD PSYCHOLOGY - The study of child behavior and guidance.
- ABNORMAL PSYCHOLOGY - The study of irregular mental phenomena.

PSYCHOMETRICS - The science of measuring psychological variables.

PSYCHOSIS - Severe mental illness.

RESPONSE - Any reaction that depends on stimulation. In individuals this is usually muscular or glandular. In groups it may be varied.

SCIENCE - (Also Natural Science) A system of knowledge derived from observation and experiment. Utilizes the scientific method.

SCIENTIFIC METHOD -
1. The problem is defined.
2. All available information pertaining to the problem is accumulated.
3. A hypothesis is developed. This is an assumption which seems to be true.
4. The hypothesis is proven (or disproven) through experiment.
5. The end result should be the ability to accurately predict actions and reactions.

SOCIAL SCIENCE - (1) Those mental or cultural disciplines which are concerned with the individual as a member of a group. (2) This group of disciplines includes sociology, anthropology, economics, political science, and psychology. Other fields are sometimes included. (3) There is some questions as to whether or not the "social sciences" are in fact sciences in that it is difficult or impossible to apply the scientific method in these areas.

SOCIETY - (No single generally accepted definition) A self perpetuating group possessing its own more or less distinctive institutions and culture.

SOCIOLOGY - The study of man in groups. This includes the various institutions which man has created and the changes which occur in these institutions.

STIMULUS - A unit of sensory input. May be on an individual or group basis.

BIBLIOGRAPHY

Bennis, W.G. et al. 1968. *Interpersonal Dynamics.* Homewood, Ill.: Dorsey Press.

Calhoun, C.C. & Finch, A.V. 1972. *Human Relations for Office Workers.* Columbus, Ohio: Charles E. Merrill.

Cartwright, D.S. & Cartwright, C.I. 1971. *Psychological Adjustment.* Chicago: Rand McNally.

Carvell, F.J. 1970. *Human Relations in Business.* New York: Macmillan.

Chapman, E.N. 1972. *Your Attitude is Showing.* Chicago: Science Research Associates.

Chase, S. 1956. *The Proper Study of Mankind.* New York: Harper & Row.

Clark, K. 1967. *Dark Ghetto.* New York: Harper & Row.

Coleman, James C. 1969. *Psychology and Effective Behavior.* Glenview, Ill.: Scott-Foresman.

Edwards, H. 1970. *Black Students.* New York: The Free Press.

Erb, E.D. & Hooker, D. 1971. *The Psychology of the Emerging Self.* Philadelphia: F.A. Davis.

Haas, K. 1970. *Understanding Adjustment and Behavior.* Englewood Cliffs, N.J.: Prentice-Hall.

Horton, P.B. & Hunt, C.L. 1972. *Sociology.* New York: McGraw-Hill.

Knowles, M. 1961. *Leadership Series.* Washington, D.C.: Leadership Resources, Inc.

Levy, R. 1969. *Human Relations, A Conceptual Approach.* Englewood Cliffs, N.J.: Prentice-Hall.

Levy, R.B. 1972. *Self-Revelation Through Relationships.* Englewood Cliffs, N.J.: Prentice-Hall.

Miner, J.B. 1969. *Personnel and Industrial Relations.* New York: Macmillan.

Montagu, A. 1964. *Man's Most Dangerous Myth*. New York: World Publishing.

Moore, R. et al. 1964. *Evolution*. New York: Time-Life.

Pfeiffer, J.W. & Jones, J.E. 1971. *Structured Experiences for Human Relations Training*. Iowa City, Iowa. University Associates Press. (Three Volumes.)

Poland, R.G. & Sanford, N.D. 1971. *Adjustment Psychology*. Saint Louis: C.V. Mosby.

Rohrer, W.C. 1970. *Black Profiles of White Americans*. Philadelphia: F.A. Davis.

Scheibe, K.E. 1970. *Beliefs and Values*. New York: Holt, Rinehart and Winston.

Sagarin, E. (Ed.) 1971. *The Other Minorities*. Waltham, Mass.: Ginn & Co.

Tannenbaum, A.S. 1969. *Social Psychology of the Work Organization*. Belmont, Calif.: Wadsworth.

Williams, Roger J. 1967. *You Are Extraordinary*. New York: Random House.

Winter, G.D. & Nuss, E.M. (Eds.) 1969. *The Young Adult*. Glenview, Ill.: Scott, Foresman.

Young, W. 1969. *Beyond Racism*. New York: McGraw-Hill.